KEEP
CALM
AND
CARRY
ON

THE LEAGUE OF
EXTRAORDINARY
GENTLEMEN

BLACK
DOSSIER

DAILY BRUTE

SPIES!

APPALLING SCANDAL OF MISSING DOCUMENTS

NATIONAL REGISTRATION

IDENTITY CARD

HOLDER'S NAME AND REGISTERED ADDRESS

DO NOT ALTER

Surname......................................

Other Name.................................

Address......................................

....

WARNING:
YOU WILL BE
TOLD HOW
AND WHERE
TO USE IT.

NATIONAL REGISTRATION No.

AIHD	8	4

Date of Issue
JULY 1948

IF FOUND RETURN TO MINILUV

THE LEAGUE OF EXTRAORDINARY GENTLEMEN: BLACK DOSSIER. Published by America's Best Comics, LLC. 888 Prospect St. #240, La Jolla, CA 92037. THE LEAGUE OF EXTRAORDINARY GENTLEMEN is ™ and © 2008 Alan Moore and Kevin O'Neill. America's Best Comics is a trademark of America's Best Comics, LLC. All rights reserved. William Bunter character used with permission of IPC Media. The stories, characters and incidents mentioned in this magazine are entirely fictional. Printed on recyclable paper. America's Best Comics does not read or accept unsolicited submissions of ideas, stories or artwork. Printed in U.S.A. SECOND PRINTING.

Standard Edition
HC ISBN: 978-1-4012-0306-1
Variant Edition
HC ISBN: 978-1-4012-1710-5

SC ISBN: 978-1-4012-0307-8

Jim Lee, Editorial Director

John Nee, VP—Business Development

SPECIAL THANKS:
Michael Moorcock
Steve Moore
Norman Wright

3-D section effects
created by Ray Zone

3-D EYE TEST

PROLOGUE: Bayswater Road, London, 1958.

EVENING, JACK.

YOU'VE SOON GOT THIS PLACE SHIP-SHAPE AGAIN. ALL THE POSTERS GONE, I SEE.

AYE, WELL, THAT WERE ANNIE'S DOIN', THAT.

HA HA. MRS. WALKER'S NO *SOCIALIST*, THEN?

IS SHE 'ECK. NO, LAD, STRAIGHT AFTER ELECTION SHE 'AD ALL CAMERAS TOOK OUT, THE LOT.

TO BE HONEST, I RECKON SHE'S AFTER MOVIN' BACK UP NORTH. SAYS OUR ROVIN' DAYS ARE OVER.

NOW, WHAT CAN I GET YOU?

I'LL HAVE A VODKA MARTINI OVER ICE, THANKS, JACK. OH, AND STIR THAT, IF YOU WOULD.

OTHER-WISE IT BRUISES THE ALCOHOL.

RIGHTO.

WELL, NOW.

I CAN'T SAY I REMEMBER LOOKING LONGINGLY AT YOU IN HERE BEFORE, AND I'M SURE I WOULD.

REMEMBER, THAT IS.

I'M SORRY?

WERE YOU TALKING TO ME?

I WAS CERTAINLY TRYING TO. MY NAME'S JIMMY, BY THE WAY.

I WONDERED IF I MIGHT BUY YOU A DRINK?

I DON'T THINK SO.

Bash Stree

ASIAN FLU

RAMPA YOBS

OH, COME ON. YOU DON'T KNOW ME.

NO. AND I DON'T LET UNKNOWNS BUY ME DRINKS.

SORRY, CHUM, BUT YOU'RE OUT OF LUCK.

WELL, I'LL BE DAMNED.

WAIT!

mlp mlp

WAIT A MINUTE!

LOOK, JUST HANG ON A SECOND...

RITAIN RESUMES SPACE PROGRAM—
Captains Morgan Dare and Logan APPOINTED —
SAY

FIGHTER DIES

LOOK, IF YOU'D JUST GIVE ME A CHANCE....

OH, FOR GOD'S SAKE! I TOLD YOU, I'M NOT INTERESTED IN NOBODIES.

NOW LEAVE ME ALONE.

WHAT MAKES YOU THINK I'M A NOBODY?

LISTEN, CHUM, I'M JUST BACK FROM A TOUR OF AMERICA.

LOCAL BOYS DON'T IMPRESS ME ANYMORE.

OH, SO YOU'RE IN SHOW BUSINESS?

YES, AS IT HAPPENS!

AND I EXPECT YOU'LL PRETEND YOU'RE A.... A SPACE PATROL-MAN OR SOMETHING?

WELL, NO. ACTUALLY, I'M A SECRET AGENT.

AS IT HAPPENS.

HA HA HA!

WELL, THAT'S NOT VERY SECRET, IS IT? TELLING ME?

I COULD BE AN INFILTRATOR FROM RUSSIA OR MECCANIA OR SOMEWHERE.

OH, NO. YOU'RE MUCH TOO PRETTY FOR THAT.

BESIDES, IF YOU WERE THE SECRET AGENT, YOU'D BE FOLLOWING ME.

OH, COME **ON**. YOU DON'T REALLY EXPECT ME TO BELIEVE YOU'RE A SPY?

Hmmm.

WELL, WHAT WOULD IT TAKE TO **CONVINCE** YOU?

I DON'T KNOW. YOU'D HAVE TO SHOW ME SOMETHING TOP SECRET, I EXPECT.

NOT THAT YOU **COULD**, I'LL BET.

DON'T BE SO SURE.

IN FACT, I'LL GO ONE BETTER. I'LL **TAKE** YOU SOMEWHERE TOP SECRET IF YOU LIKE, MISS...?

O-O'QU ODET O'QU

M-M STA NAN 'OOD

OODLES IT IS.

LISTEN, THIS PLACE REALLY IS TOP SECRET, BELIEVE IT OR NOT, SO NOT A WORD TO ANYONE, EH?

TAXI! OVER **HERE**!

PPES

L-LOOK, JIMMY, YOU'RE REALLY NICE AND EVERY-THING, BUT I'M NOT SURE ABOUT THIS...

NONSENSE! YOU WANTED PROOF, YOU'LL GET IT.

FOR HIRE

DRIVER? VAUXHALL, PLEASE.

BLUEPOOL For Your Holiday

IS WATCHING YO

WOW!

IN MANY WAYS, [MILIT]ARY INTELLIGENCE [WEL]COMED THE AIRSTRIP [ONE] PERIOD FOLLOWING [THE] WAR IN 1945.

NOT ME. ALL THAT ANTI-SEX LEAGUE RUBBISH.

WHEN O'BRIEN BECAME PARTY HEAD IN '52 THINGS GOT EASIER, BUT I'M STILL GLAD HE'S GONE.

NOW ENGLAND CAN GET BACK TO NORMAL.

TO JUDGE BY YOUR WANDERING HANDS, IT ALREADY HAS.

ISN'T THAT VAUXHALL EMBANKMENT UP AHEAD?

FREEDOM IS SLA[VERY]

[DEP]RESSED? [OF C]OURSE, IT'S [BEIN]G RENOVATED [AT T]HE MOMENT.

WE'RE CONVERTING IT BACK TO ITS OLD USE, AS A BASE.

WH-WHAT IS IT?

MILITARY INTELLIGENCE HQ.

NATURALLY, THAT'S NOT WHAT O'BRIEN'S PREDECESSOR RE-CHRISTENED IT.

NO? SO WHAT DID THE OLD REGIME CALL THIS PLACE, THEN?

THE MINISTRY OF LOVE.

OOH, JIMMY. ALL THESE *THINGS*. THEY'RE *EVER* SO MYSTERIOUS!

Mm. THEY WERE KEPT IN STORAGE DURING THE B.B. YEARS.

COME ON. ALONG HERE...

Th-THIS IS WHERE ALL THE SECRET *FILES* AND THINGS ARE KEPT?

AND WHEN IT WAS THIS *MINISTRY* PLACE, WHAT DID THEY DO HERE THEN?

OH, YOU KNOW.

THIS AND THAT.

HERE. TAKE A LOOK FOR YOUR- SELF.

Uh.... I, um....

JIMMY, WHAT IS ALL THIS?

WE'VE HUNG ON TO A FEW THINGS FROM THE OLD REGIME.

THIS PLACE. A SPECIAL VILLAGE IN *WALES*...

J-JIMMY, I DON'T LIKE THIS.

WELL, THAT'S YOUR HARD LUCK.

WHAT? DON'T...

Unnn...

SWEET-HEART?

ARE YOU ALL RIGHT?

Oh, FINALLY!

I HAD TROUBLE GETTING A CAB FROM HYDE PARK. I...

GOOD LO[R]... WHAT DID [YOU] DO?

WEL[L]... WHA[T] DO Y[OU] THIN[K]?

whur... WH-WHAT HAPPENED...?

OH, SHUT UP.

YOU'RE A LITTLE SHIT, JUST LIKE YOUR GRANDFATHER.

M-MY GRAND-FATHER? WH-WHO THE HELL ARE YOU?

NONE OF YOUR BUSINESS.

GOD, IS THIS WHAT IT'S COME TO? THE BRITISH ADVENTURE HERO?

PATHETIC.

UUAGHH!

...ooughh...

OH, JUST LEAVE HIM. LET'S FIND WHAT WE'RE AFTER AND GET OUT OF HERE.

WRETC[HED] LITTLE S[HIT.] A LOYAL PA[RTY] MEMBER [I'LL] BET.

Huh. IF HE'D BEEN GERMAN, HE'D HAVE BEEN LOYAL TO HYNKEL.

NOW, WEREN'T THE FILE ROOMS SOMEWHERE AROUND HERE, BACK BEFORE THE WAR?

HERE WE ARE.

IT'S THE RIGHT SECTION, TOO. ISN'T THE TRAVEL GUIDE THEY BASED ON US?

NOW, IF WE CAN JUST FIND...

ah.

...ASHING. NOW WE CAN FIND OUT HOW MUCH VIPERS LIKE LIME ACTUALLY *KNOW* ABOUT US SINCE WE SEVERED CONNECTIONS.

RIGHT, THEN. LET'S GO.

IT'S TOO BAD WE CAN'T DIG UP SOMETHING ON THEIR NEW BOYS, LIKE DRAKE AND MERES. IF WE...

HOLD ON. WHAT ON EARTH IS...

Mu fuffin barfuf!

Mu fuffin *BARFUF...*

BHAA!

AOW!

AOW, bloody *HELL...*

YOU KNOW, YOU'D BE A LOT LESS TROUBLE IF WE JUST *SHOT* YOU.

Ghuhh:

Huh. AND WHAT'S *THIS*, WHEN IT'S AT HOME?

HARD TO SAY, MELTED LIKE THAT.

ANOTHER TEN YEARS, THEY'LL PROBABLY HAVE IRONED THE BUGS OUT.

PROBABLY.

COME ON. HOPEFULLY, MY CAB'S STILL WAITING.

Ah, GOOD. YOU HUNG ON. COULD YOU RUN US OVER TO BROOKGATE NEXT, PLEASE?

OOH, I'D BE *THRILLED* TO, DARLING!

HOF IN, Y TWC

"GLAMCABS"?

WELL, DON'T ASK *ME*. IT WAS JUST THE FIRST TAXI I SAW.

OH, DON'T GIVE ME THAT. YOU CAN MANAGE TO BRING A SALACIOUS QUALITY TO PRACTICALLY *ANYTHING*.

I MEAN, "OODLES O'QUIM."

HONESTLY.

GENTLEMENS LAVATORY

OH, I DON'T KNOW.

TELL YOU THE TRUTH, I THOUGHT THAT WAS RATHER FUNNY.

HA HA HA!

YES, I SUPPOSE IT *WAS*, REALLY. AND DO YOU KNOW, HE DIDN'T BAT AN EYELID?

HE MUST MEET WOMEN WITH NAMES LIKE THAT ALL THE *TIME*.

HA HA HA HA.

...ERE ...U GO, ...E. KEEP ... CHANGE.

...MY, *YOU* ...WO LOVE- ...IRDS ARE ...ME TO ROOST ...ARLY.

IS THE NIGHTLIFE *REALLY* SUCH A BORE?

OH, HELLO, MR. KISS.

NO, IT'S JUST WE'RE LEAVING FIRST THING TO- MORROW, TO TRAVEL UP NORTH.

LEAVING? OH, WHAT A *SHAME!*

AND FOR THE *NORTH,* TOO! DREAD- FUL.

WHEREVER SHALL I FIND TWO YOUNGSTERS SO KNOWLEDGEABLE ABOUT THE *MUSIC HALL?*

OH, YOU'LL SURVIVE, I'M SURE.

...YES, ...PECT

Ah WELL, CHEERIO, THE PAIR OF YOU AND *GOOD LUCK...* WHATEVER YOU'RE *REALLY* UP TO.

HAHA.

...GOOD- ...IGHT, ...R. KISS.

EERIE BUGGER. DO YOU SUPPOSE HE'S *REALLY* A MIND-READER?

ONLY ON STAGE. NO, HE WAS JUST JOKING.

COME ON. LET'S GET INDOORS.

QUICK, WE'LL SETTLE THE RENT IN THE MORNING. LET'S GET TO OUR ROOM BEFORE...

OOH, IT'S *YOU* TWO!

GOR, YOU GIMME A TURN.

OH. HELLO, MRS. C.

LOOK, WE'RE OFF TOMORROW. IF WE PAY TO THE MONTH'S END, IS THAT ALL RIGHT?

Huhur. COURSE IT IS, DUCKS.

OH. RIGHT. WELL, H-HERE'S A TENNER, THEN. THANKS FOR HAVING US.

OH, YOU'D REMEMBER I'D 'AD YER DEARIE.

WHERE YER GOIN' ANYROAD?

A-ACTUALLY, WE WERE HEADED UP NORTH. WE... WE'VE GOT *FAMILY* THERE.

ANYWAY, WE WERE SORT OF PLANNING ON AN EARLY NIGHT, SO...

Mum?

WOSSUP? I'M TALKIN' TO THE *LODGERS*...

Franky was doin' me, so our Jerry shot him with some fink, and now we fink 'e's dead again.

JERRY YOU LITTLE *SHITE* YOU WAIT TILL I COME IN THE...

I'LL FRY YOUR KNACKERS AND 'AVE 'EM FOR BREAKFAST, MY LAD!

YOU SEE IF I *FUCKING* DON'T!

KIDS! YOU GOTTER *LARF*, AIN'T YER?

WELL, I 'SPECT I BETTER LET YOU GET TO BED.

UP THE BUM AND NO BABIES, AY, DUCKS?

The posters on the wall read:
HOLBORN EMPIRE · LEWIS AND CLARK · Professor DONNOL · ARCHIE RICE

THEATRE ROYAL · LIFTING YOU ON WINGS OF SONG · FEVVERS · ALSO APPEARING Mr. J. STARK THE INCREDIBLE INDIAN RUBBER MAN · COMEDY of ARTHUR e washboard TKINS ER DRAWERS

BLOODY HELL. THANK GOD WE'RE GOING TOMORROW. THAT APPALLING WOMAN!

YES, SHE'S QUITE AWESOME, ISN'T SHE?

LET ME GET THIS TART'S OUTFIT OFF...

IT OBVIOUSLY WORKED. WE GOT THE DOSSIER.

WELL, I NEED A JOLLY GOOD WASH, WITH THAT SWINE PAWING ME.

MAKE US TEA, WOULD YOU?

RIGHT YOU ARE.

YOU KNOW, IF WE'RE LUCKY, NOBODY WILL FIND HIM UNTIL MONDAY.

Hmmm. OR PERHAPS HIS TIE-CLIP'S REALLY A RADIO.

T DO YOU AN?

I MEAN WE HAVE TO ASSUME THE TRAIN STATIONS WILL BE WATCHED FROM TOMORROW.

WE'D BETTER HITCHHIKE OR SOMETHING.

I EXPECT YOU'RE RIGHT.

YOU THINK THEY'LL SEND ANYONE AFTER US?

THEIR DOSSIER'S GONE. THEY'LL SOON WORK OUT WHO MUST HAVE TAKEN IT.

SO YES.

OF COURSE THEY'LL SEND SOMEONE AFTER US.

I MEAN, WHEN WE BROKE FROM BRITISH INTELLIGENCE AFTER THE WAR, THEY MUST HAVE ASSUMED WE WERE *DEAD.*

Mm. OR THAT WE'D NEVER *EXISTED.*

"UNPERSONS." WASN'T THAT WHAT THE REGIME CALLED PEOPLE LIKE US?

PEOPLE THEY'D REVISED OUT OF HISTORY, LIKE CHARACTERS WRITTEN OUT OF A STORY.

FRANKLY, YOU WERE LUC[K]Y BUYING THOSE OLD *MUSIC[?]* POSTERS. IT'S A WONDER TH[E] PARTY HADN'T *DESTROY[ED]* THEM.

YES. YE[S,] THEY, WE[RE] A FIND[?]

BUT THEN THAT WAS A STREET MARKET FOR THE *PROLES,* LIKE MRS. C.

THE REGIME LET THEM BE, MOSTLY.

THEY COULD HAVE *REBELLED,* THEN?

YES, BUT WHY *WOULD* THEY?

GOD, YOU MEAN THAT GHASTLY STATE-APPROVED *PORNSEC* STUFF?

THEY WERE LEFT ALONE, GIVEN CHEAP GIN, CHEAP PORNOGRAPHY...

OH, SO YOU'RE *FAMILIAR* WITH IT, THEN?

WELL, I SAW [THE] 'ADVENTUR[ES OF] JANE' SERIES WAS EVERYW[HERE.]

BASE[D ON] SOME WO[MAN'S] DIARIES[, I] SUPPOS[E.]

YOU DON'T SERIOUSLY IMAGINE JANE'S *REAL?* SOME CHAP AT PORNSEC WROTE THE *LOT,* I BET.

HERE, IS THERE ANY HOT WATER LEFT?

A BIT.

WELL, LET'S HAVE IT IN HERE, BECAUSE THIS IS BLOODY *FREEZING.*

COMING UP.

DO YOU WANT THE TEA IN BED, WHEN IT'S MADE?

THAT'D BE NICE. WE CAN TAKE A LOOK AT THE DOSSIER.

OOH. OOH. YES, THAT'S LOVELY AND WARM.

THAT'S PLENTY, DARLING, THANK YOU.

YOU'RE ELCOME.

HERE, I SAW IN THE PAPER THAT THEY'RE RESUMING BRITAIN'S *SPACE PROGRAM* AFTER THE B. B. YEARS.

Really?

O YOU EMEMBER EETING AVOR?

GOD, YES. SIXTY YEARS AGO, IN THAT LITTLE *CRICKET CAP.*

DO YOU THINK TODAY'S ROCKETS STILL USE CAVORITE?

PROBABLY.

Brrr. WHERE'S THAT *TOWEL?*

Mmm. That's better.

WASN'T VERY *TANNED,* WAS HE, FOR SAYING HE'D BEEN TO JAMAICA EARLIER THIS YEAR.

Hm?

WHO ARE WE TALKING ABOUT?

IMMY THAT LESTED ME ARLIER.

APPARENTLY HE WAS THERE SPARRING WITH SOME MAD *SCIENTIST.*

ISTANT ELATIVE F OUR OLD MEHOUSE VERSARY, M TOLD.

GET AWAY! I WONDER IF *HE'S* STILL ALIVE? THE DEVIL DOCTOR?

NOT IN ENGLAND. THE PARTY PURGED LIMEHOUSE IN '48.

NOW, WHERE'S THAT *DOSSIER?*

PROBABLY IN YOUR BAG, WHERE YOU LEFT IT.

I'VE GOT IT. IT'S...

OH, THAT'S A NUISANCE. SOME THINGS TUCKED INSIDE HAVE FALLEN OUT.

NEVER MIND. PROBABLY NOTHING IMPORTANT.

WELL 'S ALL IN HANDBAG NYWAY.

GOD, LOOK AT THIS *DUST!* THIS HASN'T BEEN OPENED FOR *AGES.*

YOU WERE RIGHT. OBVIOUSLY, THEY'D LOST INTEREST IN US. THEY...

GOD, ALLAN! YOUR FEET ARE LIKE *ICE!*

Sorry.

LET'S HAVE A LOOK, THEN.

DON'T BE SO *IMPATIENT.*

ALL RIGHT, ARE YOU SITTING COMFORTABLY?

THEN WE'LL *BEGIN.*

THIS WARN YOU

THIS
WARN
YOU

Docs after in oldspeak. Untruth, make-ups only. Make-ups make
THOUGHTCRIME. Careful. Supervisor rank or not to read. This
warn you. THOUGHTCRIME in docs after. SEXCRIME in docs after.
Careful. If self excited, report. If other excited, report. Everything
report. Withhold accurate report is INFOCRIME. This warn you. Are
you authorised, if no stop read now! Make report! We know. Careful.
Any resemblance, living or dead, is ungood. Make report. If fail make
report, is INFOCRIME. Make report. If report made on failing to
make report, this paradox. Paradox is LOGICRIME. Do not do anything. Do not fail to do anything. This warn you. Why you nervous?
Was it you? We know. IMPORTANT: Do not read next sentence.
This sentence for official inspect only. Now look. Now don't. Now
look. Now don't. Careful. Everything not banned compulsory.
Everything not compulsory banned. Views expressed within not
necessarily those of publishers, editors, writers, characters.
You did it. We know. This warn you.

CONTENTS

ON THE DESCENT OF THE GODS by Oliver Haddo (1941)
...and's foremost practitioner of the occult documents the pedigree of our world's extra-
...nsional and supernatural visitors.

TRUMP featuring The Life of Orlando (1953)
...csimile edition of the popular British boys' periodical, containing a pictorial
...raphy of the transvestite fantasist and charlatan.

FAERIE'S FORTUNES FOUNDED by William Shakespeare (1620)
...rst folio of the great dramatist's final uncompleted play, a prelude to The Tempest
...describes Queen Gloriana's founding of Prospero's men.

THE NEW ADVENTURES OF FANNY HILL by John Cleland (1912 edition)
...biographer of the notorious wanton provides a sequel, detailing her association with
...Gulliver Group. SEALED SECTION. RESTRICTED ACCESS.

GULLIVER'S TRAVAILS (1794)
...re eighteenth century political caricature referring to the Gulliver Group, as
...cted by the era's leading satirist, Humphreys.

A TRUE AND FAITHFULL MAPPE OF Ye BLAZING WORLDS (1695)
...ng a chart of the apparently non-existent archipelago between Britain and the Arctic,
...ted by the Duke of Milan and amended by the later Gulliver Group.

SHADOWS IN THE STEAM by Campion Bond (1908)
...n excerpt from his biography, 'Memoirs of an English Intelligencer,' the former spy
...cusses the formation of the Murray Group in early 1898.

THE NAUTILUS, A CUTAWAY SCHEMATIC (1955)
...o reprinted from boys' weekly TRUMP, we herein reproduce a finely rendered cross-section
...the late Captain Nemo's famous vessel.

A PROSPECTUS OF LONDON (1901)
...iew of England's capital as it was in the time of the first Murray Group, with many
...dmarks that pertain to their extraordinary exploits.

BULLETINS FROM BEYOND (1899-1913)
...tcards and correspondence among the Murray Group in the years following the failed
...tian invasion of 1898.

THE SINCEREST FORM OF FLATTERY (1909-1924)
...account of the attempts by France and Germany to duplicate the Murray team with their
...ensembles, Les Hommes Mysterieux and Der Zwielichthelden.

WHAT HO, GODS OF THE ABYSS by the Rt. Hon. Bertram Wooster (1928)
...famed English diarist recounts an incident from the late 1920s, involving both the
...ond Murray Group and an incursion into this world by eldritch and primeval entities.

WHEN THEY SOUND THE LAST ALL CLEAR (1939-1945)
...ost-war compilation of reports concerning Murray and her comrades' doings both here
...abroad during hostilities, with illustrations from ephemera of the period.

THE WARRALSON TEAM (1946-1947)
...taining an embarrassing account of the attempt to duplicate the Murray Group's success
...the war's aftermath, under the leadership of WAF heroine Joan Warralson.

THE CRAZY WIDE FOREVER by Sal Paradyse (1957)
...celebrated American 'beatnik' writer, in this chapter from his recent novel, narrates
...encounter between Murray, Quatermain and the mysterious Dr Sachs.

DIRECTOR'S SUMMARY (1957)
...sing comments by the current 'M' relating to the current status of the Murray Group
...light of its abscondence after 1945 and subsequent break with Military Intelligence.

RESTRICTED
OFFICIAL USE ONLY

ON THE DESCENT OF GODS

BY OLIVER HADDO

The following, distilling as it does a longer and more comprehensive treatise published in *The Solstice,* vol. 1, VI, concerns mysteries that will prove impermeable to all save those adepts who have fully understood my own *Liber Logos*, dictated by an unseen presence in Cairo during 1904. For this reason, I have where possible simplified the matters discussed in the text, so that they may prove lucid to the scrutiny of a more generalised and averagely intelligent readership.

From scant surviving ancient accounts and certain material received during magical investigations, it is possible to ascertain that the earliest contact between our material realm and the various ethereal 'dimensions' adjoining it probably occurred some millions of years ago, perhaps shortly after the emergence of proto-human life upon this planet. The celestial energies concerned are referred to in the Book of Genesis as 'Elohim,' a curious Hebrew word that is at once masculine, feminine, and furthermore plural, and which may be broadly understood in context as 'the gods and goddesses,' our inference surely being that the Christian God of the Old Testament was perhaps one amongst many such divinely manifested beings. This is not to deny that all such manifestations may ultimately be the various emanations of a single monotheistic source; simply to point out that the processes involved may be at once more subtle and more complex than is generally allowed in the philosophies of our conventional religions.

These earliest 'gods and goddesses' and their subordinate hosts of angels may, of course, have procreated in some fashion amongst or between themselves, while texts such as the apocryphal Book of Enoch are suggestive of limited interbreeding between a specific rank or class of 'angels' and the earliest human beings. We may only speculate with regard to the offspring that may have resulted from such couplings, but it is sufficient to remark upon the implication of a thriving, viable celestial stock, a divine lineage with the potential for both evolution or degeneration over the successive æons, as with earthly and material bloodlines. In any event, it would seem that some several millennia after the arrival of the generally-benign biblical Elohim on our material plane of being, there transpired a new incursion into our dimension, by less welcome entities.

These beings, termed collectively 'Great Old Ones' i[n] century alchemist Johannes Suttle's fine translation of the mystic Abdul Alhazred's seminal *Necronomicon,* would to be powerful djinns or malignant spirits originating in a material dimension (sometimes misidentified by neophyte mere physically-existent planet) known as Yuggoth. While f numerous to list exhaustively within the space available fo report, these alien deities or quasi-deities included extra-tary horrors such as the monstrous, tentacle-adorned Kutul seething exemplar of primal chaos known as A-Tza-Thoth grotesquely fertile and many-limbed she-goat called [Shub-] Niggurath; and the sinister Hermes-like messenger N'Yala-T[ot] Ep, sometimes referred to as 'The Haunter of the Dark.' B[y] time of the arrival of these entities in our dimension, it w[ould] seem that Earth's prior occupants, the Elohim, had by some[mea-] sure seen their power diminish or degenerate across the æo[ns] that they were mere 'Elder G[ods'] unable to resist invading forces wit[h] ease that may have viously been expe[ri-] Even so, all the [Great] Old Ones were ev[entu-] ally either bani[shed] from our plane of b[eing] or else magically im[pris-] oned in empow[ered] locations such as [the] vast sunken city R'[lyeh] found in 1926, s[ome] distance from the c[oast-] line of New Zealan[d.]

During their te[nure] in our world, bri[ef in] cosmological te[rms,] these alien or qlipp[othic] interlopers w[ould] appear to have, m[uch] like the Elohim, interbred betw[een] themselves and also to have sired a great variety of half-b[reed] monsters on the human population, such as Tibet's noisome degenerate 'Tcho-Tcho' people, or the fish-like humanoids covered on an island close to Zara's Kingdom in the South Pa[cific.] As with the mooted offspring of the Elohim themselves, we construe that down the æons various further interbree[ding] would most certainly occur, accounting for the widely va[ried] plethora of monsters, chimeræ and spirits that have popu[lated] human history and folklore ever since.

As for the former Elohim themselves, having suffered a dec[line] to become mere senescent Elder Gods, it would seem that [their] power had been further diminished by their war against the [ter-] rible Great Old Ones. By the time of the earliest, since-lost hu[man] civilisations before and during the great Ice Age, when Britain

ned to both the Arctic kingdom of Hyperborea and to con-
al Europe by an ice land-bridge, Earth's first 'gods and god-
' had seemingly degenerated into relatively brutish, unso-
ated tribal deities such as the war-god Crom, once wor-
ed by Cimmerians in what is modern Scandinavia. At the
ime, though exiled or imprisoned, the Great Old Ones still
ued to exert an influence and to command a worrying mul-
of worshippers. Thus it appears that there were still per-
to be two distinctly different trans-substantial 'clans,' if you
ith one benign and one malignant, that both governed and
ed all the various doings of the human race.

the end of the great Ice Age (also the end of the so-called
rborean Period'), with what are now the British Isles made
ate for the first time from continental Europe, references to
-cults and Kutulu-worship seem to all but vanish from the
ological record. One of the few surviving cultures in this
storic world was that of the immensely cruel and decadent
bonéan Empire, Melniboné being the name by which the
n Isles were known immediately following the disappear-
of the continental land-bridge. The Melnibonéan worldview

d seem to have been essentially Manichean in that central to
s the notion of two diametrically opposed and adversarial
s in the universe, Lords of Order warring endlessly with
s of Chaos, with these evidently serving as the mythopoeic
s into which earlier eidolons such as Crom, the Elohim and
Great Old Ones had by this time either evolved or declined.
emporary geologic evidence suggests that shortly prior to
commencement of the Neolithic era, some decisive, cata-
nic conflict between these two rival forces must have taken
e, the Lords of Order perhaps making a last-ditch attempt to
terbalance powerful and dæmonic Lords of Chaos such as
h and Pyaray. Whatever the true circumstances, the result
devastation unimagined until last year's development and
onstration by our allies in America of the Atomic bomb. If we
conceive an entire global war conducted using such devices,
we may have a comparison to the destruction visited by this
ibonéan-period disaster on humanity, driven back to wear-

ing skins and dwelling in caves, just before conventional history
begins.

Some few thousand years later, by the Bronze Age, we may
readily suppose that the surviving residue of these opposing
astral forces might have undergone the ordinary mutations of
time and heredity, resulting in their transformation to the Titans
and other prototypical giant races that populate the early stages
of the world's nascent mythologies. These would themselves, in
time, give rise to a great plethora of more sophisticated and more
fully realised spiritual energies, which became known as the classic Gods when manifested to various cultures of the ancient
world.

It is with the various pantheons of this classical era,
Babylonian, Greek or Egyptian (the gods of which great civilisations would often appear to be the selfsame energies, as con-
ceived of by markedly differing cultures), that we first have some
sense of divine agenda in the interactions between mankind and
its deities. Though just as profligate in fathering half-human
chimeræ as their celestial predecessors, the more cultured deities
inhabiting the Greco-Roman world would seem to have had
some occulted purpose in their promiscuity, perhaps a hoped-for
hybrid race that would one day conceivably provide a bridge, a
bond between the mortal world and the ethereal, by means of
which communion between man and his divinities may be more
certainly effected. This concealed agenda is born witness by the
brief proliferation of the half-god race of Heroes, men like
Hercules or Aeneas, just as surely as the Trojan War in the tenth
century B.C. bears witness to the failure of that divine project. If
Homer is to be believed, the siege of Troy was engineered by the
Greek gods and goddesses, deliberately, to cull the Hero race
that they themselves had sired decades before, only to see the
hybrids' human qualities collapse beneath the weight of their
divine inheritance, producing vain and strutting homicidal monsters. It may be that it was the tragic end to this preliminary
experiment that caused the gods to gradually withdraw from our
material domain across the coming centuries, perhaps to ponder
some new strategy by which their aims might be achieved. The
different pantheons retreated, one by one, into their home-
dimensions, so that eventually only the Teutonic deities
remained, these being obliterated by some terrible ethereal
catastrophe during the sixth century A.D., an event mirrored in
our own realm by collision with a piece of meteoric rock, dust
darkening Earth's skies for several years.

All of these various god-races, like the Elohim and the Great
Old Ones that had come before, left our material realm a legacy
of færies, demons, sprites and monsters that would eventually
become so populous that during the grim, lightless depths of the
Dark Ages, they held sway across the greater part of both Europe
and western Asia. As if to provide a harbinger of these forthcom-
ing pagan centuries, the great magician Merlin was born into
Roman-occupied British society at some time during the late
fourth century, reputedly during the period when Emperor Julian
had declared Britain to be officially a pagan nation. Merlin, of
course, rose to become a trusted counsellor during the brief but
laudable Arthurian period, only disappearing with the fateful ter-
mination of that era, circa 470 A.D. By this time England had
become an ogre-ridden, færie-haunted place, thanks largely to
the influence exerted by King Arthur's close blood relative, the
færie queen Morgana La Fey. Morgana's claim of a connection to
the English Royal bloodline would eventually come to be of some
importance more than a thousand years thereafter, in the reign of
King Henry VIII.

By this time, during the Renaissance, a magical or færie influence upon human affairs of state was tolerated and accepted,
even openly encouraged. With the half-realm (or perhaps the
fractional dimension) of the Færie homeland recognised as an
important sovereign state, and its titular then-monarch Oberon
the First perceived to be the head of a most venerable Royal

household, it seemed only natural that Henry VIII should take King Oberon's second cousin, the distinctly Færy-blooded Anne Boleyn, with her protuberant eyes and a sixth finger on each hand, to be his second wife. The offspring of this controversial union, it need not be said, was England's alabaster-complexioned, reportedly unearthly monarch, Queen Gloriana the First, under whose remarkable reign, commencing in 1558, the magical and otherworldly came to play a greater part within the English worldview of those times, as they did in the majority of alchemy and magic-obsessed nations throughout Europe. It was Gloriana who appointed, from the outset of her rule, the noted alchemist and sorcerer Johannes Suttle as her court astrologer, a decision of far-reaching consequence.

Johannes Suttle (or 'Subtle'), said to have been born variously in Worcestershire or else into Italian aristocracy, was probably in his late thirties when he embarked upon magical service for Queen Gloriana. Residing at a house in Mortlake by the churchyard with his wife Doll and a distinguished, if notorious, fellow alchemist called Edward Face, Suttle performed with Face the groundbreaking experiments that would provide the basis for much of the Art of Magic, as it is practiced in the west up to the present day. Suttle had, while still a boy of tender years, apparently met the famous European occultist John Faust, and shared Faust's predilection for the art of diabolic conjuring. With Face's aid, Suttle established contact with innumerable ranks of spirits which purported to be those same human-loving angels mentioned in the Book of Enoch. In his investigations of these beings and the immaterial 'æthyrs' they inhabit, Suttle came across a female entity of dreadful power, who would come to obsess various later occultists, this being the Thessalian witch-goddess called Smarra.

With the death of his beloved wife in the first years of the seventeenth century, Suttle is variously reported to have entered a decline and died at Mortlake, tended by his surviving child, Miranda, or according to some accounts to have gone into self-imposed exile on a distant island, with his life prolonged by sorcerous means. What is certain is that within a year of his death or departure, in 1603, Queen Gloriana herself took ill and died, to be succeeded by the fiercely puritanical and anti-færie King Jacob the First, devout compiler of the now-standard King Jacob Bible. This new king organised bloodthirsty purges of the Færie race and other supernatural creatures, with the result that by 1616, Oberon's Fairyland had severed all its contacts with the human world, with England literally rendered disenchanted in direct result.

Obviously, despite disapproval from the Church and Crown, a line of individual sorcerers kept interest in the Magic Arts alive during the centuries that followed. In the late 18th century, the noted Spanish occultist Señor Don Alvarez, said to have sworn a pact with the Devil in the form of a beautiful little girl named Biondetta, carried out certain forbidden operations to establish contact with the goddess or dæmoness called Smarra, transcribing in his writings the ferocious and blood-curdling prophecies that had been ventured by that entity. Smarra, originally raised during the orgiastic and tribadic rites of the famed sorceress Medea and her sister-witches there in the ancient region of Thessaly, was also the subject of the obsessions of Germany's reputed 18th century 'Ghost Seer,' the Count Von Ost, himself a prized associate of 'the Sicilian,' who was believed to be an alias of alchemist and scoundrel Cagliostro.

My own association with this sacred, fiery female energy began in 1904, while I was on my honeymoon in Cairo. Following certain signs and omens, I had retired into a solitary study where I would be able to write down whatever messages the spirits might see fit to pass to me. The resultant work, *Liber Logos,* written over three successive occasions upon three successive days, is a most holy and perfect announcement of the terrible Aeon that is to come, with myself as its Prophet, and is in part dictated by the

goddess Smarra. This has since been published as *The B... the Word,* without a full understanding of which it is in... ble for the human race to fulfill its celestial destiny.

Briefly, the congruence between Smarra and the ... Whore of Babylon from the Book of Revelations has bee... firmed to me by mystical investigation, yielding various in... Just as the Whore of Babylon is thought to be a Christian d... ising of the Babylonian mother-goddess Ishtar, so too is S... with her name, in all likelihood being a corruption of 'Sa... another centre of Ishtar worship during the Babylonian ... Applying the art of gematria to the name of the goddess ... further confirmation. In the numerically valued alphabet ... Hebrews, we find that SMARRA is equivalent to the numb... hundred and two, with the associated meanings 'to tell gl... ings' and also 'the flesh,' both appropriate to the highly ...

alised spirit of Apocalypse. In the Pythagorean gematria ... Greeks, the name yields a number value of four hundre... forty-two, which signifies 'termini terræ,' or the end of the ... another clearly apocalyptic association. Finally, and most p... sively, according to Homeric Greek gematria, the name SM... has a value of just sixty-six, this being the mystic number ... Qlippoth, and also that of the Great Work itself. What, to th... tiated adept, could be more conclusive?

It was after the revelations contained within *Liber Logo...* I withdrew from the venerable occult organization known a... Order of the Golden Twilight, or 'Geltische Dammerung,' to ... my own magical order, the Ordo Templi Terra (O.T.T.), or C... of the Temple of Earth, which continues to investigate the c... worldly entities and territories that have lately, it would s... come to preoccupy those shaping policy at Military Intellig... If I may be of any further assistance to the government in ma... of this nature, do not hesitate to contact me at the address ... have on file, this being the Netherworld estate in Hastir... remain, yours most sincerely, Oliver Haddo.

The Word is Law.
The Law is Love.

The Life of ORLANDO

1. Gather round, kindly readers. Draw closer and I'll tell a tale like no other, of loves, wars, and empires ground down unto sand, for my name is Orlando, and I have lived three thousand years.

2. I write this by lamplight, a young man in bombed, bla London with Herr Hynkel's Luftwaffe droning above am neither young, nor, back then in 1260 BC, was I bo man.

3. Splendid Thebes was my birthplace, fair Bronze Age Greek city-state there in Boeotia. The 'Seven Against Thebes' were by then defeated, their sons yet to rise and avenge them, and all was at peace.

4. The blind seer Tiresias, cursed to change into a woma back, and companion to tragic King Oedipus, father dear sister Manto and I. She inherited his gift of prop while I inherited nothing.

5. Or so it appeared. I was named Bio then, meaning 'life', and aged ten that life changed when I sprouted male organs, becoming a boy. Neither Father nor Manto had seen *that* one coming, apparently.

6. Horrified by this reminder of his gender-changing s Father sold me as an exotic novelty to pirate slavers bou Egypt. Father later died, I heard, escorting Manto to be the oracle at Delphi.

...at a life I led amongst those rogues, tossed on the heaving ...t of the Mediterranean. What things I learned of sails ...nots, of how to curse and drink, and many other things

besides. Being a girlish boy, as I had been a boyish girl, I learned, a little, how to fight and how to love, both in a rough way. My companions thought I'd fetch a pretty sum.

...d so I did. This was 1250 BC by the current reckoning. ...e androgyny was fashionable with Egypt's ruling class, I ...ecame a favourite of the Pharaoh Usermattra, called by ...Ozymandias.

9. He was a vain, pretentious man. Some centuries thereafter, passing through that place, I saw the great stone head men speak of. It looked nothing like him, having neither his weak chin, nor chubby jowls.

...ventually, aged just nineteen and older than the Pharaoh ...his boys, I sought out new employment, drawing on my ...amongst the pirates to enlist upon on expedition setting ...or Punt, in Africa.

11. Without a seafaring tradition of its own, Egypt depended upon foreign sailors for its expeditions, with whom I found easy berth...and soon, around the Horn of Africa, found much, much more. — *Continues next week —*

The Life of ORLANDO

1. Born a girl to gender-changed Tiresias of Thebes, become a boy aged ten and sold in slavery to Egypt, in 1240 BC I embarked for Punt in Africa, by now a strong young man.

2. We'd barely landed when this changed and I found ▮ female once again, nor was I some androgynous young Feeling unsafe amongst my lusty former crewmates I es into the jungle, almost without incident.

3. For weeks I wandered aimless, living off the forest, stumbling at last upon the ancient land of Kor, in what is now Uganda. There, within a great, sky-blasted crater, I discovered a peculiar pool.

4. Bathing in its lapid, liquid flames, emerging strangely ised, I noticed old names and a map carved at its edge. not carve my name there 'til millennia later, during the u▮ Ayesha's rule.)

5. The map led me to Abyssinia, and a community of others who had bathed within the pool, who told me I was now immortal, as were they. Some, the oldest, had a sullen, troglodyte demeanor.

6. Spending decades amongst them, I finally detected this nation in myself, and moved on. I'd been Mistress Bio a▮ time, but it was Master Bion that the Abyssinian chie Memnon sent to defend Ilium.

Ilium, as Troy was then called, in 1184 BC, I first knew a conflict instigated by the gods to cull their hybrid by-, the increasingly alarming, often psychologically ble race of heroes. Those I met were pitiable, or else hate-

ful: Ajax a confused brute; Achilles a smug, invulnerable maniac; Odysseus a shifty little swine. Even Aeneas, son of Aphrodite and Anchises, whom I escaped Troy with, wasn't perfect.

, I loved him well enough. Everyone did. Son of the Love dess, Aeneas was irresistible, breaking hearts everywhere, poor Queen Dido's when, headed for Italy after Troy's fall, we put briefly into Carthage.

9. Tragedy haunted Aeneas's family. Living with them in Italy for eighty years as loyal, ageless Bion, I finally saw Aeneas's great-grandson Brutus banished for accidentally killing his father, and elected to travel with him.

1101 BC, anchored near Leogetia, Brutus went ashore save for myself. At a shrine of Diana, he dreamed the dess told him of a northern isle where he would found a ty nation.

11. So it was, some months thereafter, that we reached the place of which the Moon Goddess had spoken. Seeing its white cliffs loom majestically ahead, I knew I'd found another home.
— *Continues next week* —

The Life of ORLANDO

1. Born female in 1260 BC with my sire Tiresias's tendency for changing gender, I had emerged immortal from an African pool, and fought at Troy as Bion, comrade of Aeneas. Now it was 1100 BC, and, with Aeneas's great-grandson, young Brutus, I'd reached the northern island where a vision told Brutus he would found a mighty nation. Disappoint it was already populated by a grotesque race of giants.

2. These were subdued when Brutus's best wrestler threw their chieftain (a monstrosity called Gogmagog, or possibly Gogma-geot) over a cliff. Within ten years we'd almost wiped out the entire giant race upon that rain-swept isle.

3. Obviously, some survived, vengefully plaguing Bruta Brutus named the land) for centuries. By then, though, more female and weary of Brutain's capital New Tro Troy-Novantum), I'd moved on for pastures greener.

4. Named Bio again, I worked my passage East by means of prostitution and small fraud, settling here and there along the way. In 960 BC, aged 300, I reached Cathay, now called China.

5. As a handmaiden of the great King Mu, I travelled with unto Mount K'un Lun, where lived the goddess Hsi Wang her mountain palace guarded by a human-headed tiger na Lu Wo.

...er the King departed I remained, becoming lover to the ...Mother of the West, as the goddess was known. She'd ...d immortality by copulating three thousand men to ..., and our passions were furious.

7. Gods are exhausting, even to immortals, and finally I left, travelling back to Italy under my new, Latinate name, Vita, which also means 'life.' Unbelievably, I'd tarried there two centuries, time passing differently amongst deities.

...wo millennia later, I heard that the ruthless Ugandan ...ortal Ayesha, finding herself incarnated in China and ...g a power-base, had somehow contrived to both kill and ...ce Hsi Wang Mu, ruling there on K'un Lun, now called

Hes or Fire Mountain, in my lover's stead. Though I confess the fact with shame, that is one fight I should have liked to witness. However, returning to my own tale...

...eturned to Italy in 774 BC, I found the new-built city ...e, and met its founders, wolf-reared Romulus and Remus. ...tical twins, I slept with both accidentally, prompting ...ulus to murder his brother.

10. Luckily, this tragedy coincided with fresh stirrings down below. Vita became Vito, escaping Rome unnoticed. Decades later, the scandal forgotten, I joined Queen Semuramis's Indian expedition, seeking Eastern tranquility. *Continues next week*

The Life of ORLANDO

1. Made dual-gendered and immortal by astounding quirks of fate, I was 560 years old when, in 700 BC, I enlisted in the army of Babylon's Queen and founder Semuramis, then engaged in conquering India. As manly Vito, veteran of Troy, I routed enemy war elephants, becoming the Queen's for military advisor, though never her bedfellow since she te to execute these the following morning. Presumably, I s her better alive.

2. Decades later, Semuramis seduced her own son and successor, allegedly becoming divine upon her death. After that I moved on, fighting for Persia against Greece at Marathon in 490 BC, afterwards wandering the region.

3. Thus it was in Macedonia around 334 BC I met with a bitious, somewhat mad young stable-hand named Alex, w across the next decade or so, I helped to subjugate most o world.

4. At sea-monster-plagued Alexandria in the 320s, I suggested Alexander build a bathysphere so that the creatures might be scrutinized and sketched, allowing the construction of great metal likenesses along the Alexandrian shoreline. These giant effigies scared off the monsters most effectively, where Alexander claimed all credit for the scheme. The iron le thans, much weathered, still endure today as a beach amusement area for tourists and their children.

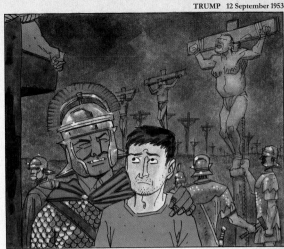

ortly after Alexander's death I became Vita again, spend-
he next two hundred and fifty years reading my way
gh the great library at Alexandria, with Ptolemaic
t's fabulous although incestuous culture spread around me.

6. Male once more, I returned to Rome in 70 BC, my fling with
its founders now forgotten. Embroiled in slave revolts, I
escaped punishment by simply declaring "I'm Vito," everyone
else apparently being named "Spartacus."

nding myself in the Roman Army, I accompanied Julius
ar during 55 BC when he invaded Britain, as Brutain had
me. Troy-Novantum was now squalid tribal hovels, whose
aric inhabitants successfully resisted our incursion.

8. Eleven years thereafter back in Rome, Caesar having been
assassinated, I became a soldier of Marc Antony during his
affair with radiant (albeit pungent) Cleopatra and the pair's
disastrous battle with Augustus, at Actium.

ollowing Actium, I retreated into Egypt with the defeated
rs, Augustus's men in hot pursuit. Antony and Cleopatra
ed themselves, their soldiers massacred when the pursuing
ps arrived. Fortunately, having become female, I was spared.

10. That was 30 BC. Female for barely three decades, by 1 AD,
as Vito, I fought Teutons on the Empire's northern frontiers.
Regrettably, in 1200 years, I'd become very good at war.

Continues next week

The Life of ORLANDO

1. Immortal and transsexual, twelve hundred years old by the first century AD, I'd seen Rome's emperors come and go. In 30 AD, slimy, child-molesting Tiberius was succeeded by the ruthless (although undeniably sane) Caligula.

2. Stuttering, skulking Claudius followed, who, in 43 AD more invaded Britain, this time successfully. Serving u him as Vito, I found Britain a depressing place, transferri Naples with Nero's succession.

3. In 79 AD I sailed from Naples with the famed scribe Pliny's expedition to Pompeii, its citizens recently killed by an eruption of volcanic gas. Fearing further outbursts, I stayed aboard ship, thus narrowly escaping Pliny's fate. Shaken, I relocated to volcano-free lands near the Black Sea where, in 100 A became apprentice to great Appolonius of Tyana, and th the charlatan snake-cultist, Alexander of Abonoteichus.

4. By 150 AD I'd become lovely Vita once again and, after Alexander made certain advances, had defected to his rival and stern critic, the sage Lucian, with whom I journeyed accidentally to the Moon, our ship transported by a monstrous waterspout. Returned to this world, I endured the reign of r Heliogabalus around 200 AD, and by 363 was greatly chee when Emperor Julian officially declared Britain a pa nation.

Returning there, enjoying the new myth-soaked atmo-[sph]ere, in 376 AD I was seduced, embarrassingly, by a most [cha]rismatic thirteen-year-old boy. Irresistibly persuasive, [alle]gedly son to the Devil, his name was Ambrosius Merlinus.

6. In 410 Rome withdrew, empire collapsing, while Ambrosius and I watched noble Uther's Cornish kingdom take its place. Forty years later, with Merlinus in his eighties, certain marvel-lous events established a new monarch named Arturus.

[A]h, Arthurian Britain, quite as wonderful as is supposed, [but] yet within two decades foundered dismally, with Merlin [ent]ombed by a sorceress, Arturus slain in battle with his [wro]nged child Mordred on Salisbury Plain. I knew them all: knew sweet Guenevere; half-witted Percival; knew awesome, monstrously ugly Lancelot. Male once again, as Vito, I fought alongside them in that final battle (from which, incidentally, I salvaged Arthur's sword).

That was 468 AD. Re-christening the blade 'Durendal' to [dis]guise its misappropriation, I abandoned Britain to barba-[ris]m, plagued by ogres, giants, and faeries governed by [Ar]thur's half-sister, dread Morgana. A dark aeon had begun.

9. Twenty years' wandering brought me to Denmark, where as sword-for-hire I took employment with King Hrothgar of Hierot, seemingly troubled by a monster, which I assured him I could handle. *Continues next week*

The Life of ORLANDO

1. Over 1700 years old and temporarily male, 490 AD found me at Hrothgar's court in Denmark, where I encountered Grendel, a rampaging monster, and thereafter Beowulf. I'm still not entirely sure what Beowulf was, exactly.

2. A decade later, in 500 AD, I accompanied the hero Sieg who, except for being suicidally brave, had no other pers ity traits whatsoever. It was through him, however, that I glimpsed higher, ethereal realms.

3. These territories, that modern science might term other dimensions bordering ours, whilst strictly speaking outside Time, nevertheless have histories and conflicts as tumultuous as those of this material world. In the terrestrial year 568 AD,

for instance, I beheld the end of the Teutonic gods at narok, a cataclysm mirrored in the Earthly realm by a sion with a weighty meteoric rock, its dust veiling the hea for three years.

4. During this endless Fimbul-Winter, when it seemed the moon had been devoured, I made for France, where in 764 AD I joined the knights of Charlemagne under the more contemporary-sounding name of Roland.

5. In 778, beset by Saracens while in the Pyrenees, vetera Troy and Marathon, my sword Durendal flashing, I fough when all save I were slain. Impressed, my foes eventually b me join them.

a Saracen, with Roland mispronounced 'Orlando', in
d I met the Caliph Haroun Al Raschid and his beguil-
ncubine Scheharezade. More devastatingly, I also met
e of my protracted life, a mariner named Sindbad.

7. Near thirty blissful years we were together, 'til he left on that
eighth voyage from which he never would return. I moped
almost a century in Baghdad, until Haroun's grandson Al
Wathik Be'llah became Caliph.

amed with Caliph Vathek as he was more lately known,
g him build the palace Alkoremi in Samarah and accom-
g his trip up the Fakreddin Valley to the hushed black
es of Ishtakar, the genii-haunted catacombs beneath

them. Here I witnessed Vathek bargain with the demon Eblis
for a vision of Hell's treasures, whereafter his heart burned
eternally. This seemed unfair, since frankly, Hell's treasures
were rather…suburban.

at was around 900 AD. I was still wandering the Holy
when the Crusades began nearly two centuries later. Ad-
g the Crusaders' outfits, I again switched sides, fighting
side legendary Prester John and others.

10. In the 1190s, I helped Blondel and his minstrel underground free Richard, called the Lionheart, from prison. Enjoying my new name, I'd by then sworn to be Orlando all my
extraordinary days.   *Continues next week*

The Life of ORLANDO

1. Despite surviving 2,450 years already, man and woman, sometimes I feared that those beastly Middle Ages simply wouldn't end. Even Robin Hood's Merry Men, encountered in 1197 on returning from the Crusades, seemed miserable.

2. Mainland Europe was no improvement. In 1307, once again and become William Tell's assistant while h his apple trick on tour, we were everywhere beset by Da monsters, trolls and Dire-Wolves.

3. Culture-starved, by 1450 AD I had settled in Constantinople, throne of learning, where I made my living as a dancer, studying by day. Unfortunately, only three years later the Byzantine capital fell to the glowering Ottoman hordes of Mehmet the Second, ending Byzantium's empire after a mere the years. Along with other scholars, I fled west to Italy, along as many books and manuscripts as I could carry.

4. Thus I started the Renaissance, a sublime relief after those gloomy centuries. I posed for Leonardo, even though I was becoming a man at the time. I remember he kept asking me why I was smirking.

5. Travelling through Europe, in 1530s Prague I was ap ticed to the sorcerer Johannes Faust, whereby I renewe acquaintanceship with Helen, whom I had not seen since We chatted, though this irritated Faust and Mephistoph

...n afterwards, the Doctor was approached by a preco-... thirteen-year-old nobleman from Italy, seeking occult ...ction. Faust being otherwise engaged just then, I accom-...the boy back to Milan. His name was Prospero.

7. Duke Prospero's companion during youth, I went with him in 1558 to England, where he was made Court Astrologer to newly-crowned Gloriana, England's Queen, daughter of brutal Henry VIII and faerie half-breed Nan Bullen.

...arged by prescient Gloriana to inaugurate a mighty ...e after her death, Prospero resided in Mortlake under the ...Suttle, with wife Doll Common and fellow alchemist ...rd Face. Meanwhile I languished, bored, in London.

9. When his wife died, grieving Prospero took daughter Miranda to an island, not to return until 1610, when he assembled Gloriana's prophecied 'League.' This included otherworldly Christian, whom we rescued from a madhouse in 1678.

...ver time, this group embraced such notables as beloved ...ish aristrocrat Quixote, impoverished sea-captain Robert ...nuch, and ravishing courtesan Mistress St. Clair. With ...stian and deathless Prospero, flanked by his spirit-

creatures, we made a formidable ensemble. Though originally devised by Gloriana and her spymaster Jack Wilton for reasons unexplained, this league, in one form or another, would be my companions for the next few centuries. *Continues next week*

The Life of ORLANDO

1. Almost 3,000 years old by 1696 AD and currently a man, I'd taken up with an engaging crew of misfits, as originally proposed by England's faerie monarch Gloriana prior to her death in 1603. I accompanied their last adventure, ferrying an ailing Prospero back to the spectral Arctic 'Blazing W where he took leave of us forever. His last words, at the of that shimmering mirage, were 'Follow me.'

2. Since Gloriana's death and subsequent King Jacob's vicious purges of the faerie race, enchantment had been scarce in Britain. Fairyland withdrew contact entirely in 1616, the same year that noted biographers Shakespeare and Cervantes died.

3. With Prospero gone and our league disbanded, E seemed dull. I roamed the world, even revisiting Kor in and its magic pool, this time carving my name on the there beside it: 'Orlando.'

4. Returning to Britain in 1740, I found a new band of adventurers formed in my absence, this time numbering unlucky mariner Lemuel Gulliver, trapper Natty Bumppo, libertine Mistress Hill, dual-natured clergyman Dr. Syn and the resourcefull Blakeneys amongst its members dow decades. I stood by them through Brobdingnag's Giant and helped them in their subterranean adventures, fi them worthy successors to the mantle of Prospero's men ing aided Percy Blakeney during France's revolution, entury's end I frequently accompanied him, Marguerite nny on the trio's annual sojourns through erotic Europe, r weeks spent in twilit Horselberg being most memorable.

6. With the remarkably elderly Gulliver's demise in 1799, the league once more disintegrated. I spent much of the nineteenth century in France as companion to either superhuman aesthete Fortunio, or ambiguous Mademoiselle de Maupin.

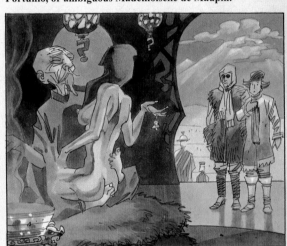

found me female, travelling in Tibet where, at the mon-So Sa Ling, I was captured by Bon sorcerers, who used eadfully, but didn't make me into ointment, as they did men.

8. Escaping, I reached the azure Mount Karakal and dragon-blazoned Shangri-La, where I was learning yoga from a willing lama when interrupted by an English couple who were undertaking expeditions in the area.

pair, Allan and Wilhelmina, turned out to be agents of nglish Crown, affiliated to the latest incarnation of the previously led by Prospero and Gulliver. It transpired we uch in common, and they were the most delicious

company as we returned to England via the North Pole, having many grand adventures on the way. I was finding this modern world most agreeably entertaining. *Concludes next week*

The Life of ORLANDO

1. Ancient and of varying gender, I contributed enthusiastically to Wilhelmina's 20th century team. In 1910, male again, I strived alongside her, Allan, the thief Raffles and occultist Carnacki to avert disaster at King George's coronation.

2. In 1913, assisting the team against French counterpar Hommes Mysterieux, I nearly died battling the albino, Z in pounding rain atop the Paris Opera. Clearly, this ne tury was as dangerous as any other.

3. It was certainly as warlike. Having some military experience, I fought for Britain in World War One, as did my colleague, penitent bandit A. J. Raffles, who'd lose his life during the conflict. At the Battle of Mons, I was lucky enough to see Agincourt's phantom bowmen aidin English. One ghost claimed to recognise me, though I think that I was even *at* Agincourt. Who knows? Pe I was.

4. After the war, I'm afraid I spent the 1920s enjoying myself. I belonged to poor Agatha Runcible's set. We knew the Woosters, the Claytons, Jay and Daisy, absolutely everyone. It was all such smashing fun.

5. The 1930s, less so: throughout the decade one coul stormclouds gathering. With Mina, Allan and othe friends, I revisited the Blazing World and the Polar v beyond, where we made some important allies.

1939, of course, the dictator Adenoid Hynkel had ⦚ the world into a new and even more destructive war. ⦚ keep abreast of changing times, I mastered aeronau-⦚ enlisted in the Royal Air Force, flying with aces such as Bigglesworth, Hebblethwaite, and visiting yank G-8 (who seemed, frankly, bonkers). Shot down over France I escaped back to Blighty to find my comrades missing in action, their headquarters deserted.

⦚ is 1943. My tale is almost over, while outside the air-⦚ ntinues. I know that Allan and Mina are alive some-⦚ and expect that I shall see them, sooner or later.

8. As for myself, I was three thousand two hundred and three years old last week, and I endure. I saw London founded, hewn with Trojan blades, and now see it flattened by German incendiary devices.

⦚ witnessed cities beaten to their knees, fought all our ⦚ ss wars, seen millions slaughtered, peerless cultures ⦚ ed by History's thumb, and, all things considered, ⦚ n't change a moment. I was Bio, I was Vita, and where human life went, there went I. It was a very great adventure, and I am proud to have been a man; to have been a woman. To have been Orlando.   *- The End -*

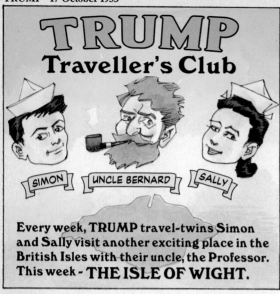

TRUMP
Traveller's Club

SIMON   UNCLE BERNARD   SALLY

Every week, TRUMP travel-twins Simon and Sally visit another exciting place in the British Isles with their uncle, the Professor. This week - THE ISLE OF WIGHT.

HURRAH! THE ISLE OF WIGHT! LET'S GO TO THE AMUSEMENTS!

YES, UNCLE! DO SAY WE CAN!

WHEN THE FAMOUS INTERPLANETARY ZOO IS HERE AT BLACKGANG CHINE? WHAT NONSENSE!

YOU SEE, CHILDREN? MOST OF THE CREATURES WERE BROUGHT FROM THE SPACE CENTRE NEAR BIRMINGHAM. THEY'RE AS SHY AS YOU ARE.

HA HA! LOOK AT THE FUNNY TRALFAMADORIAN! HE'S WAVING!

H-HE SMELLS OF SOMETHING BAD.

THEN WHAT ABOUT THESE FRIENDLY LAZUNES? THEY CAN BE TAUGHT TO SPEAK, AND MY JACKET'S ELBOW PATCHES ARE MADE FROM THEM!

UNCLE?

WHAT'S THAT GREEN MAN IN THE TYRE DOING WITH HIS OTHER TWO HANDS?

OH, HE'S PROBABLY KNITTING.

LET'S HURRY ALONG AND WATCH THEM THROWING LIVE ELEPHANTS TO GORGO'S MOTHER INSTEAD!

N-NOT ME, UNCLE BERNARD!

I'LL JUST STAY IN THIS NICE GARDEN HERE, AND PLAY AMONGST THE BUSHES!

⌇CHUCKLE!⌇ CAREFUL, SIMON! THOSE "BUSHES" ARE TRIFFIDS!

EEEIGH! KILL ME!

H.W.— This next item's inte
allegedly an unfinished, priv
printed folio edition of Sha
who R.K.C. tells me you e
back at Greyfriars. B
G.O'B

Printed in England and published every Saturday by Junior Publications Ltd., Trump House, Shoe

The True Chronicle of
certain Mysterious Events
in and around the Courte of
our Noble QUEEN GLORIANA,
in a playe called:

FÆRIE'S FORTUNES FOUNDED

By William Shakespeare

AT LONDON

Printed by I. R. for B. Bond and are to be sold
by private subscription only, inquiries at
his offyce near St. Austin's Gate
1620

DRAMATIS PERSONÆ

PROSPERO, Duke of Milan
ORLANDO, Squire to Prospero
GLORIANA, Queen of England
SIR JOHN WILTON, Servant to the Crowne
SIR BASILDON BOND, an Intelligencer

MASTER SHYTTE
MASTER PYSSE
Gatekeepers

DOGROSE
GORSE
LOVE-LIES-BLEEDING
Færies

Færie's Fortunes Founded

Actus Primus, Scena Prima

e gates of *Nonsuch Palace. Master Shytte* and
aster *Pysse occupying separate gate-houses.
Master Shytte enters from gate-house left.*

Shytte.

nother morn in this hag-ridden land,
   Our right Queen Mary sickened to her
   crypt
d leaves enthroned a changeling in her ſtead.
hy does the very Sun himself not shy
his ascent, from such iniquity?
me, Master Pysse! Throw off your lively
eets!
w let us be about our grudging round.
ake faſt these gates at Nonsuch and besides
ep safe she that deserves salvation leaſt.

Enter Master Pysse from gate-house right.

Pysse. Insiſtent Shytte, again you waken me.
ck'd from such dreams as break my heart to
it.
time to come, when all the world's set right
d sweet young Jacobus the Scottish King
grown, brought to his juſt inheritance.
hat are these wraiths and sorc'ries caſt aside
ith her alike, whom are we made to call
ur good Queen —

Shytte. Hold thy water, Pysse! Speak not
r cog, leſt like her kin she come when hailed.
t us to work, such dang'rous chat put by.
fficient in our private thought that these
pinions spilled delinquent out our mouths
re truth, like all we speak, true as our names!

Pysse. Ah, noble names indeed, everywhere
own.
ntinels at the gates of Life itself.
is said that all men, commoner and King,
re come into this world 'twixt Pysse and
ytte.
t hold! I see two travellers bide near,
ayhap the lords Her Majesty awaits.

Shytte. I mark them now, the both
ar damn'd as she.
he elder is a Duke sailed from Milan.
ne Prospero, an alchemist by trade
ith not yet forty Summers 'neath his cap
nd sure to catch the Queen's lascivious eye;
he other man, scarce more than boy, his
uire.
rlando called, that gossips would unpick,
eclare not man at all but rather dame
manly guise, or thing of doubled sex.
will-gill or a child of Herm - yet soft!
hey tread too soon upon our whisperings.

Prospero and Orlando enter left.

Prospero. Good squire, behold the palace of
None-Such.
Nor such as mortals shall e'er see again.
Where are we fetched from Italy to meet
Fair Gloriana, England's færie Queen.
But what is this? Can this drab pair ahead
Be their lords Bond and Wilton we were told
Should meet us here, and hence accompanye
Our joining with her gracious Majeſty?

Orlando. Why, my lord Prospero, I will
confess
I have heard much of England's poverty
Yet did not think to see her thus reduced,
Her lords with gunny-sack for ermine swap'd.
I shall inquire, and know the truth of it.
If these be the intelligencers we
Were told to seek, or else tares in our way.

to gatemen

Hail, fellows. We are come from far Milan
In search of two within your Queen's employ
As spies, and we would know if you are they.

Shytte. Do we spy? Aye, we spy, we watch,
we see.
Have we not each these two balls in our heads?

Pysse. More than are in your britches, if the
tales
That coſter-men speak everywhere be true.

Orlando, aside. They jeſt with me, I shall
give jibe for jibe.

to gatemen

Why, sirs, you make me teſty with your talk
And teſt me sorely. Must I teſtify

As once did I in ancient Rome with hand
On heart, or other muscle made for love?
Though I be fair and orchidaceous, know
My *Orches* are in place, may orchestrate
A love-air sweet as any orchestra
Might play at the famed dances of your Queen,
Reknowned, 'tis said, for her great, splendid
balls.

Shytte. Your wit fair spins my head with all
its play!

Pysse. Yet have we cudgels that shall
spin your own!

Prospero. Orlando, hold thy wounding barbs.
'Tis plain
These are but gatemen, not the ones we seek.

to gatemen
Now, gentlemen, thy cudgels put aside
Or be advised Orlando here has blade
yet keener and more practised than his tongue.

enter Sir John Wilton and
Sir Basildon Bond, right

Bond. Noble Sir Jack, 'tis our Italic guests
That we must take before the strangeling
Queen.
Already is their Latin blood aflame
And set to quarrel with the lackards here.

Wilton. Cease, men of Lombardy, in thine
affray.
Sheathe thy stilletos and restrain thy boot.
I am Jack Wilton, this Basildon Bond,
Your escorts to our fledgling monarch's side.

Orlando. I am at fault, good gatemen. You are
not
The ones for whom I, erring, did you take.

Shytte. Ho, took us, did you? Are we ta[l]
then?

Pysse. Why, hadst thou best inform [M]
Majesty
Thou took both Pysse and Shytte at Nonesw[...]
gates.

Prospero. Put off these pratings! Good lor[...]
I am come
Through many seas this audience to find
And would bright Gloriana soonest see
If here in England I'm to have my notch.

Wilton. Well said, friend alchemist, w[...]
leaden thought
Made wisdom's gold on thine alembic lips.
Come, bring your squire. Step with us throu[...]
these gates
To venture on her presence half-divine
And scrye there vasty empires' secret fates.
Let our talks be unknown, our words erase:
In Nonsuch Palace, none such did take place[.]

Curtain

Scena Secunda

Gloriana's throne-room. The Queen sits, attend[...]
by færies.

Gloriana. My pretty devils, fold thy prism
wings.
Halt now thy flutt'ring galliard and draw nea[...]
For spies and sorcerors would have my ear
To weave their schemes, whilst weave I bet[...]
things.

Dogrose. You play a higher, broader game th[...]
they!

Gorse. The spots you've reckoned ere th[...]
die are cast!

Gloriana. Fine webs of circumstance sh[...]
hold them fast.
And though they wriggle shall I have my wa[...]
To write a hist'ry that I've ten times read —
Yet hush! Methinks to hear their falt'ring trea[...]

Enter Wilton, Bond, Prospero and Orlando, le[...]

Bond. This scented atmosphere do I despis[...]
Thick with the reek of myrrh and færie mush[...]

Wilton. Say nothing. Here the very wa[...]
have wits
And ears. E'en private thought be overlooked[...]

to Glorianna
Sweet Majesty, I come, thy prince of spies
With stout Basildon Bond, in your domain

d bring the alchemist, the Milanese,
ere with his squire, the both for you to meet.

Love-Lies-Bleeding. He sweats. Sour
amonds mist upon his brow.

Dogrose. The other as milk-pudding heaves
d shakes.

Gloriana. Why, though their perspirations
k fresh lakes,
ne foreigners they bring would I quiz now.
and forward, alchemist. Stand forward,
uire.
is proposed you should positions find
my employe, the one with agile mind,
he other, agile blade to fit my hire.
ndly Duke Prospero, of you 'tis said
nat knowledge both of metals and of tides,
f stars, and of math'matic art resides,
rbits the heavens, in thy black-capp'd head.
hus should it please me that you now remain
London here, at Mortlake to the West.
secret wait my call and my behest,
hich means my sly Lord Jack might next
plain.

Wilton. Gladly, Your Highness. Good Duke
ospero,
ay I suggest, referring to thy fame,
hat here you wear another name, become
n altered personality, take guise
s one John Suttle, born in Wor'stershire,
nd subtle both in name and nature be.
hen should thy veiled utility be twinned,
oth conj'ror to Her Radiant Majesty
nd spy, a wand'ring alchemist abroad
ho might from the low countries make
port,
serving my intelligencers' band.

Prospero. What band is this, of agents
andestine?

Bond. It is an instrument that serves the
own
hrough stealth, its master my Lord Wilton
re:
s 'M', for em's but double-U disguised.
e are by letters, else by numbers masked.

Prospero. Shall I, then, newly named, be
umbered thus?

Wilton. *produces paper*
have your own appointed symbol drawn,
e, with its dotted circles like to eyes
hat glower beneath the straight line of a
ow.

Prospero. It seems like bosoms, or a brace of
ughts.
vo 'O's, within a seven bracketed.

Wilton. Then two 'O's and a seven is your
sign,
And to this mark are all your payments writ.

Prospero. They've called me Faust, for one
that I once knew,
Call me by numbers, Suttle, Prospero.
Caught at my aliases' delta now
Hang I as in a saddle-wire, a dee.

Orlando. What of I, and my part? I am unsure
If I'm to Arthur or else Martha be.

Bond. Stay at our beckon as a sword for hire
Lodged here in London, ours to fetch and send.
When not employed you may, for all I care,
Hack at a dangled Tartar's head for sport.

Gloriana. My good Sir Basildon, your words
offend.
You and my good Lord Wilton must go hence.
Leave me to salve my guests of thine offence
And to my duties as hostess attend.

Wilton. Your Majesty, forgive me my protest,
Dismiss'd with such irregularity —

Gorse. Go, or thy wits lose in our ludic maze!

Love-Lies-Bleeding. Go, or misplace recall of
thine own names!

Exeunt Wilton and Bond, right

Gloriana. We are alone. Jack Wilton fears my
games
More than the peeking pass-time that he plays.
Now, master alchemist and master squire,
Can I make my true purposes more plain,
A confidence spies' ears shall not retain,
Not England's scheme, but Fairyland's desire.
Bronz'd Duke, I see the future, so may plan
A league of champions, yours to convene.
Nor yet, but when I'm dead and 'neath the
green.

These earthly heroes, bridging Gods and man
A glorious roster that I now may sight:
The mariner, bedraggled and in debt,
Your spirits and your selves, not to forget
The courtesan, nor sweet deluded knight,
Nor pilgrim with his bundle knotted, furled,
That shall precede you to a blazing world!

Prospero. Most lovely Queen, I am confounded quite
To hear you talk, so young, of your demise.
When shall be acted, then, thy prophecies
Of this brave band? Please God it is not yet!

Dogrose. Horse-blinkered mortal, know ye not that Time
Is made in Færie's realm a single day?

Gorse. We're not yet born; our dusts long blown away,
All hours immortal in this spell sublime.

Gloriana. What Dogrose, Gorse, and Love-Lies-Bleeding sing
Is Færie truth: Time's but a painted screen
Whereon our shadows fatten then grow lean,
Reflections pale of the eternal thing.
Yet be assured that my time is not yet,
Nor 'til our sixteenth century be done
When shall a new King scorn our færie fun,
Shall bid men plough us under and forget.
But you, good Duke, have much to do ere then,
Shall live at Mortlake, study, take a wife,
Raise children, lead a fulsome earthly life
And then, bereaved, shirk from the world of men.
My foresight has you cloistered on an isle
With daughter, books and sprites of earth and air
Until such time as sailors, venturing there,
Should tell thee that I have been dead the while.
Then shall thou make for Albion to enlist
The paragons and powers I have foretold,
Your friends 'til the new century grow old,
When shalt thou disappear, as arctic mist.

Prospero. Pray hold! Fair Queen, I should not have my days
Set out before me as a butcher's roll.
May we, perhaps, not speak of sweeter things?
With such as thou beside me, bright and pale,
I would not all our talks be death or fate.

Gloriana. Thinkest me fair? Would I hear more of this,
Should not a young man's flattery despise,
Would see mine self there mirror'd in his eyes
As object fit to worship, woo, and kiss.

Prospero. Jew'ld Queen, how might I flatter such as thee
Whom Ocean called his Cynthia, his Moon?
Why art thou not that very silver'd orb
That off in far Cathay men style Chang-O.
Night's goddess, seen there when the disc full,
And near her skirts a cunny, or else hare?

Gloriana. Why, should I like a cunny-hare pet,
They are both soft and warm, and likewi quick.
How might I set its velvet ear a-prick
Or make its nose to twitch, so pink and wet?
Then should I have about me, by my troth,
That which is cunny and a-prick the both.

Orlando. *aside*
She tells it as it were a novelty,
Yet should she truly be thus twice endow'd
Then would I sympathy with this queen sha

Prospero. Nacreous, opalescent majesty,
O how thy scents and atmospheres enchant!
Pray send me not to Mortlake, there to wed,
Have children, have another life and name
When sooner would I here with thee abide,
Here in thy bow'r, white rose without compare.

Orlando. Beware, young Duke, lest th impert'nent be!
Art thou made by this Cynthia bewitched,
A moon-calf, struck whilst twin white cresce rise
Past the horizon of her bodice there?
Then have a care: though heady be her bloom
Her thorns, conceal'd, are sharp, shall stab t heart.
In my great span, since far-off Thebes have
Some few queens known, and several be besides,
That would doom milling thousands with l heed
Than they might blue a lid or paint a lash.
Fear not! How dismal might thine exile be,
In pretty Mortlake with a comely wife?
Think of me there, languish'd by Bloomsb' Park,
Sat idle, slicing at the heads of Turks!

Prospero. Good fellow, boyhood friend, th warn'st me right,
I am made lunatic by this moon's light.

to Gloriana
Glorious one, my foolish words forgive
And set me to thy bidding as thou would.

Gloriana. Go then, wise Prospero, and subtle
At Mortlake, while thine young yet aged squi
Make off, at sep'rate lodgings to retire.
In both thy dreams, see that thou lovest me.

*exeunt Prospero and
Orlando, right*

Love-Lies-Bleeding. They are well gone, and
ke the reek of man.
u had them dazzl'd, blinded in your thrall.

Dogrose. At last they hardly knew themselves
all
nd so may willingly act Færie's plan.

Gorse. How would thy mother, lushly-
agered Anne,
r thy great-uncle Oberon rejoice
o know thy scheme; know that thy cunning
oice
ifts Færie's wish since history began?

Gloriana. Dear moths, draw in thine orbit to
y flame,
r I am satisfied, would drowse and play
nd count my acts sufficient to this day,
r the advantage of my gem-tiled game.
ur kind, from other æthyrs, came before
ankind, to stamp a foot upon this Earth.
urfold, eternal, strange to death and birth,
rung up from angels or else fiends of yore,
e watch'd man born, we monsters, gods and
rites,
nd fear'd what enmities there might arise.
urselves made deities to crowd Man's skies,
r ghouls and devils to distress his nights,
e sought to make a bridge that spann'd the
vain,
awn'd heroes, half-bred gods, in this employ;

Saw them go mad, then cull'd them all at Troy,
Vowing that we should not so err again.
This league of champions that I propose,
Though not convened whilst am I in this world
Is our next try to have two realms knit, purled
Into one seamless drama without close.
Our Duke shall near two centuries survive,
Suttle at Mortlake, Prosp'ro on his Isle,
Shall found my league and keep with them a
while,
And thence into the mystery shall dive.
There is, past Britain's tip, like to a gate,
A blazing world, door to a diff'rent plane.
There Prosp'ro goes, nor shall his league
remain,
But in Time follow to another state,
'Til when the years have in their hundreds
passed,
'Til other men else women lead my band
And in this Blazing World shall take their
stand,
A bridge-head 'tween our realms secur'd at last.
Now sleep. There are dire days to come ere
then,
Our bright kind scourged by new Kings and
their men,
Burn'd out from woodland, driven off from fen,
And would I know Dream's moonlit towns
again.

they sleep

Finis Actus Primus

The present publication is an unaltered facsimile, reproducing a previously undiscovered limited first folio edition from 1620 of what is alleged to be an uncompleted final play by Shakespeare, *Færie's Fortunes Founded,* said to have been commenced by the great biographical dramatist in 1616, its writing presumably curtailed later that same year, after only one act of two scenes, by Shakespeare's death at the age of fifty-two. Although the provenance and pedigree of the preceding fragment has been vigorously disputed, the current editors of this facsimile edition have elected to make room for a brief note in which the main points raised by the foregoing piece's critics and debunkers may be answered, it is hoped conclusively.

Several commentators have suggested that the two scenes which survive of *Færie's Fortunes Founded* are unlikely to be Shakespeare's work, if only on account of the unflattering references to Queen Gloriana, who had, as sceptics have quite rightly pointed out, been Shakespeare's patron, and at least on friendly terms with her most celebrated play-write. While the present editors have no wish to refute these well-established facts, they would point out that *Færie's Fortunes Founded,* being written in 1616, was obviously commissioned a considerable while after Gloriana's death in 1603, some twelve years into the reign of Gloriana's deeply Christian and deeply resentful nephew and successor, King Jacob the First.

If the uncompleted play under discussion had indeed been written at the King's request, it is perhaps not wholly unexpected, then, that Shakespeare may have felt compelled to include sentiments that were both hostile to the late Queen, and also to the idea of færie-kind in general. Let us recall that Jacob's animosity both to his aunt and to the færie breed she represented was both fierce and deadly. Barely had the new King claimed the throne on Gloriana's death than he released an edict branding færies and associated beings as 'Devils,' or as Jacob himself put it at the time in his book *Dæmonologie,* 'That kinde of devils conversing in the earth may be divided in four different kinds...The fourth is these kinde of spirites that are called vulgarlie the Fayrie.' (III,i)

Indeed, so great was Jacob's loathing of the fairy race that his reign saw the ruthlessly efficient purges of the species from the British Isles, with the destruction of their woodland habitats. By 1616, at the time of this play's writing, there were no more fairies to be found in England, and in Shakespeare's references to the Queen's

fairy attendants as 'my pretty devils,' it may be tha[t] author was attempting to play to his royal master's [prej]udices. However, it should be observed that most o[f] piece's anti-fairy sentiment is placed into the mout[h] characters who are themselves either buffoonish, lik[e] coarsely-named and almost certainly fictitious gate[men] or else devious and duplicitous, like the spym[aster] Wilton and his chief intelligencer, Bond. (While John Francis Wilton, more commonly called Jack [was] a young adventurer who'd risen to a prominent pos[ition] in the court of Gloriana, whose existence can be [veri]fied, Sir Basildon Bond's name does not appear, at [all] in the official records of the period, and it may be [that] he, like the comic gatemen, was invented by the [author] entirely for dramatic purposes.) Perhaps by attrib[uting] such cruel views of the Queen and her attendan[ts to] such obviously unsympathetic characters, Shakes[peare] hoped to make his own true feelings plain wit[hout] offending the strict sensibilities of his royal pa[tron] Jacob.

One other, smaller, bone of some contention [that] the critics have seen fit to worry over and hold u[p as] proof that *Færie's Fortunes Founded* could not [have] been penned by Shakespeare, is the unobtrusive [refer]ence made by Prospero, during his musings on [the] many names by which he has been labelled, to 'a sa[dle] wire, a dee.' Such critics have declared the English [use] of the word 'dee' to denote a d-shaped loop of wi[re] which means objects such as weapons or canteens [may] be hung from a saddle, does not commence unti[l the] early 18th century, more than a hundred years [after] Shakespeare's demise. To these learned pontificato[rs we] would only timidly observe that many of the words [used] in the English language have been found, upon ex[ami]nation, to have their first printed usage in the wor[k of] Shakespeare. Might it not be that only the com[para]tively late discovery of *Færie's Fortunes Founde[d* has] prevented the word 'dee' from having its rightful i[nclu]sion in the Swan of Stratford-Upon-Avon's almost [omni]scient vocabulary?

There is no doubt that history will be the final j[udge] of this work's authenticity, and with that firmly in [our] minds let us, then, in conclusion, ask the reader to [put] such controversies to one side as they read and hop[eful]ly enjoy what is at very least a fascinating and [entertaining curiosity in its own right.

Sincerely,

The Editors

THE NEW ADVENTURES OF
FANNY HILL
Or, The Further Memoirs of a Woman of Pleasure

as recounted to Mr. John Cleland

LONDON:
MCMXII

My Dearest Mr. Cleland,

You are surprised, no doubt, to hear from one whose exploits were the substance of a book you wrote some forty summers gone. Given the troubles heaped upon you following that publication, might I hope that said surprise is not unpleasant, at a correspondence unexpectedly renewed after so long? I am, you may be sure, still your own sweet, young Fanny, yet the worrisome idea occurs that you, dear Mr. Cleland, must be older now if, please God, you are yet alive. You surely have not been preserved in so remarkable a fashion as have I, by methods I shall presently explain. Kindly biographer, it is my hope that these lines find you well, and young enough, at least in some part, to respond as once you did to my adventures, frankly told. You may recall when last I wrote I had just married Charles and settled to a life of wifely virtue. This was not to be. Advised by friends I soon surprised Charles at a bawdy-house kept by the elderly, infamous Madame St. Clair. Cutting him off without a sou, I sold the home that had become a grave, now, to our love, and thought that I should like to travel and forget.

Do not think me hasty in my sudden urge to journey. Rather, I was powerfully sensitive to my uncommon situation: after the release of your biography, good Mr. Cleland, my most intimate affairs were seemingly made plain to all the world. In subsequence, I had received (as have you, I am sure) both smirking admiration and rebuke, in equal measure. Seeking guidance, yet with no one sharing my condition to whom I might turn, I was thus glad to learn that the notorious Mistress Flanders was returned, a wealthy widow, from her sorry transportation to Virginia. Visiting her London residence I found a handsome, generously-made wench, fifty-and-some years of age, her situation not unlike my own, happy to share the benefits of her experience. She bade me travel broadly and love freely, though advised that readers only love a wanton if she make pretence at penitence. "Discussing love, your warmest treasure," here she gestured, "is your euphemism. Whether writ or spoke, the hand glides smoothly to it, else it lingers, tart and wicked, on the lips, the tongue." Here were our conversation's thread, sweet Molly's hand below my petticoats and all our raiment lost, yet I took home from our encounter her advice, and fresh resolve to roam the globe.

And so, in 1754, some six and twenty years of age, I set out for my foreign jaunt upon a clipper out of Bristol where, narrowly having missed the evening's tide, I was obliged to wait until the morning after, finding myself unexpectedly without accommodation. Fortunately, I fell into discourse with a former shipboard surgeon, one Lemuel Gulliver, who gallantly proposed I share his rooms above a nearby tavern, *The Admiral Benbow*. Though like Mistress Flanders he had twice my years, he made, like she, for stimulating company. He too had suffered scandals from dissemination of an over-candid memoir, but suggested that such bawdy tales might be more widely tolerated if there were a comic or fantastical approach to their recounting. We then passed the night with an agreeable discussion of my host's many adventures and the keepsakes that remained from them, such as the miniature-made garden of the Zipangese kind that he kept there as a window-box and habitat for tiny, bare homunculi; a dozen lewd and acrobatic natives he had smuggled out from distant Lilliput. He also demonstrated a device from science-crazed Laputa, to invigorate tired skin, that I found endlessly delightful. I sailed next day, thinking I should not meet my friend again.

And now, my dear biographer, I must narrate one of my most surprising misadventures hereto. We were not far sailed from England when our ship fell foul of pirates, captained by one Clegg, whose youth belied his infamy. I dare not think what fate befell my fellow travellers, for the handlings I received were stern and vigorous. Taken aboard the buccaneer's ship *Imogene*, you may imagine that I was the subject of much ribald commentary and not a little solitary ardour in the rigging. This persisted until Captain Clegg himself elicited my name, and on the instant swore himself my most sincere admirer, having read my exploits in your own account, sweet Mr. Cleland, which I gathered had been something of a favourite with the *Imogene's* discerning crew. With my credentials thus established, the young brigand's attitude towards me was entirely changed, so that he was made more concerned for my well-being. During a fierce tempest, he insisted that I be lashed to the wheel for my own safety, sheltering my body with his own, close pressed. He even offered me a tour of the Malaccan Straits, suggesting that he take me up the southeast passage, although I declined, asking instead to be set down somewhere in Europe.

Thus I came eventually to be put ashore in Rotterdam, greatly surprised that I had not had my considerable fortune taken from me by my roughneck captors. As it was, the gallant Captain Clegg insisted I be paid a proper wage for what he called my services aboard the *Imogene*, and to this end had passed a hat amongst the crew for their donations. I thanked them sincerely, though it seemed to me I had not done a stroke. From Holland, then, I next made my way south by carriage into Germany, where near the border shared with France I came at last to Micromona, a peculiar country that is ruled by women and where men are kept only as slaves. Affecting to be angels plunged from Paradise, the Micromonan ladies claim to get themselves with child by rattling the branches of a certain tree brought there from Heaven, though in truth this is accomplished with the necessary substances delivered by means of a large cake-icing mechanism, or syringe. Indeed, my hostesses took me to see a novel type of dairy-farm whereat the vital raw ingredient concerned was humanely collected and then taken off for future usage. I remained in Micromona for perhaps a month, then travelled on.

And so it was that I reached Horselberg, called sometimes Venusberg, beneath which
mountain in a wanton, twilit sprawl exists the realm of amorous Queen Venus. In exquisitely suggestive ornamental gardens spread about the tunnel-mouth that let into this perfumed underworld itself, I paid my coachman, not in coin, though to my way of thinking
very generously, and then ventured alone down that pellucid passageway under the hill,
the very mound of Venus. Here there flapped nocturnal butterflies of a prodigious size,
their vast sails stained with vivid arabesques richer than all the tapestries of the Orient.
Having attained the cavern's furthest end, I came into the country proper and was greeted
in a most surprising although not unwelcome fashion by the Queen herself, surrounded
by her playful courtiers. Later, when we were by ourselves, Her Majesty revealed the
means by which the huge and lovely tunnel-moths were fed, anointing our most sensate
parts with fragrant treacle as we slumped together on a lush and velvet grassy slope. Soon
we were each attended by some half-a-dozen of the gorgeous, fluttering things that
cleaned us with long sable tongues, curled up like gentle whips, and lulled us to exhausted slumber with the soft petticoat whisper of their wings.

I would not have you think, kind Mr. Cleland, that my time there under Horselberg was in
entirety consumed by the pursuit of sybaritic pleasures, for I had occasion also to
acquaint myself with many lively and inventive works of literature, and was indeed
myself allowed to make in some small means a contribution to the Arts. Residing in one
wing of the extensive palace was an illustrator, a Marquis named Dorat, kept there at the
Queen's behest as painter and official portraitist by Royal appointment. Taking something of a shine to me, the talented Marquis suggested I should pose for his next composi-
tion, which he told me was intended to imply that sacred union which exists between the
various and innumerable living things in God's creation. Supine upon a decorative
chaise-longue, I was to represent humanity, while standing for the kingdom of the beasts
we had the Marquis' own firmly-built hunting dog, a puddle-hound (so called for their
wet-looking coats) named Franz. Years afterwards, revisiting that land, I showed my dear
friend Marguerite the illustration that resulted, although she, disdainful, did not recognise my likeness, whereon I thought better of confessing.

Time passed so oddly there beneath the mountain that it scarcely seemed to pass at all. For all I knew it was yet the late months of 1754, or early on in 1755 at worst, myself not yet quite twenty-seven years upon the world. One afternoon, the Queen and I reclined together in the lavender-oil scented waters of her marvellous bath-house, fashioned in what I construed to be an Ottoman or else Byzantine style, where we were suffering the quite delicious ministrations of the 'minnows' Venus kept there for this very purpose, although also for their decorative worth. These slipped and darted into each submarine cranny, nibbling where the dark weed drifts slow and luxuriant beneath the water, so that when the bath-house doors burst rudely open, interrupting us, it took both Venus and myself some several moments to become again composed. Recovered from our crises, we discovered our intruders to be an outlandish crew led by my former intimate acquaintance Mr. Gulliver, who, though it seemed to me but some few months since our encounter was now frail and in his dotage, ninety years or more in age. Apparently, the year was 1793, so when my new companions finally left Horselberg, I travelled with them.

What an adventurous gang they were! Besides the now-elderly Gulliver, the group includ-ed a tatterdemalion smuggler who, beneath his mask, proved to be yet another old com-panion, namely Captain Clegg, himself aged to a silver-haired man of some five and sixty years. A huntsman from America, one Mr. Bumppo, was a younger man, but had a rather cocksure manner that I did not care for, and it was with the two youngest members of the fellowship, a very pretty English couple called the Blakeneys, Marguerite and Percy, that I found the deepest friendship. Our extraordinary band, I learned, were catspaws of the British Crown, and I had many startling exploits in that company. Upon the westerly American peninsula called Brobdingnag, inhabited by giants, we became embroiled in wars between Brobdingnagians and displaced colossi, descendants of the towering Pantagruel, come from Utopia in the southern seas. Once, whilst attempting to negotiate a truce in secret with a sympathetic giantess, her hostile spouse returned home unexpect-edly, whereupon we were hid about her person. Horrifyingly, her husband chose this moment to insist on conjugal activity, so that we, with our coach and horse, were only spared when, evidently, he decided on some other method of ingress at the last instant.

Our other outings were no less alarming nor intriguing, as when we investigated the extensive subterranean territories of the Earth in 1796. I was at this time, I suppose, a septuagenarian, although despite having commenced the normal processes of aging once again on leaving Venusberg, I was to all appearances a comely girl of not yet thirty. In our underground adventures we clashed with the legionnaires of Roman State 'neath northern England, and in monstrous vaulted caves below what we supposed to be the town of Newcastle or thereabouts, we first encountered the strange, stygian civilization of the Vril people or 'Vril-ya' as they called themselves. It was Marguerite and I who fostered an amicable relationship between our league and this remarkable winged breed, after the mutual misunderstandings and hostilities of our first confrontations. Snatched aloft and kidnapped by a female of the species, we were taken to a wide bowl of carved pumice raised atop a stalagmite, that served as nursery to her adolescent young, with Marguerite and I delivered up to these as morsels or confectionary treats. We quickly found the Vril to be a loving, noble folk, whose kisses had the power to thrill or heal, and learned why they are sometimes called 'the coming race.'

Many were our adventures of a like to this, although these ceased in 1799 upon the death of our beloved mentor, Lemuel Gulliver. He had, to all appearances, died in the arms (and bedchamber) of a sometime addition to our league, the changeable, immortal warrior Orlando, who was female at the time of Gulliver's demise. With Captain Clegg and Mr. Bumppo having quitted our ensemble sometime previously, it was left to Orlando, with the Blakeneys and myself, to see acted our leader's often and fondly expressed wish that he be buried on the isle of Lilliput, so that his grave, a shallow mound to us, should be a grassy hill where youthful Lilliputian lovers should have fine, gay picnics on the gentle slopes. Distressingly, the case of wine we'd brought with us to toast our comrade's passing fell instead into the tiny hands of Lilliput's native community, and was enough to make them wildly drunken in their thousands. A dreadful, seething orgy then broke out, in which it seemed that every member of their population, young or old, was feverishly involved, so that with clothing ripped or chewed to ribbons, it was only by the grace of Providence that we were able to crawl free and find our ship again.

With wise and kindly Gulliver dead, it seemed that those of us remaining were not much inclined to risk our youthful health and beauty in pursuit of dangerous adventure, and preferred instead idle devotion to the pleasures of the senses. For some years, resting between exploits, Percy, Marguerite and I, sometimes accompanied by glamorous Orlando, had been holidaying at some of the European continent's most amatory resorts, including Horselberg, and it was on a tour of such agreeable locations that we now embarked, our services no longer, it would seem, required by our shadowy paymasters in England. One erotic paradise we often visited was the delightful kingdom of Tryphême upon the coast of the Mediterranean, close to the Balearic Isles. Here, in a society refreshingly made free of all shame and pretence, all actions which do not distress one's neighbours are allowed, and women are encouraged to go naked save for silver sandals and a yellow scarf upon their heads to shield them from the constant sunshine. Men, less pleasing to the eye, go dressed and have felt hats to spare them from the blaze of noon, although for reasons that are presently obscure to me they never wear these, but rather elect to carry them by hand from place to place.

Another favourite destination was Cockaigne, often called also Cocaigne or Cuccagna, a small inland country at the edge of Germany that we were told could also sometimes be an island when the vast, wide lake surrounding it was not dried up. Here, all was dedicated to contentment, so that there were laws where anyone found working might be gaoled. The physical delights of love were not neglected, with the city's wondrously decorated palace library containing helpful charts of the venereal postures and positions, alongside such classic writings as *The Thirty-Two Gratifications*. But it was in pleasures culinary and gastronomic that Cockaigne excelled, with almost every building and its furnishings or fittings made from the most sweet and toothsome delicacies. The hotel where customarily we stayed was an enormous and elaborate moulded aspic that let in the light through walls of colourful and delicately-flavoured gelatine. Percy and Marguerite would roll and slide upon the sticky counterpane of icing spread across their gateaux bed, while in a sunken tub of hard-glazed golden honey-crystal I would frolic with Orlando in the warm and swirling cocoa-au-lait pouring from the peppermint-cane spigots. Thus we passed the years until perhaps 1802, when I decided to return alone to Venusberg.

Do not infer from this, good Mr. Cleland, that I spurned my comrades, nor they me. Indeed, we parted as the very best of friends and all expect that we might see each other soon enough when next they venture in their journeying to Horselberg. I left my lovely Marguerite and Percy to enjoy (particularly Percy, I suspect) the newly-altered nature of Orlando, who was by this time become a man again, and went back a girl still little more than thirty years of age to that sublime town underneath the hill, where I knew I would not again grow old. In truth, time is so queer within this place that generous Queen Venus introduced me to her best-beloved, the chevalier Tannhauser, though I had seen with mine own eyes the sprouting traveller's staff some way from Horselberg said to commemorate the knight's death in the thirteenth century after Our Lord. Think kindly of me, Mr. Cleland, endlessly at sport and fun amidst the perfumed gardens of this glorious, time-forsook domain, and if these further memoirs should afford you but the slightest surge in your former affections for me, then be assured that I am pleased, and that moreover I remain your own, true

Fanny Hill

The Most Popular Tall-Tale Teller in the Tavern.

Farmer George, in his cups, delights the Ale-House with his merrie nonsense, rewarded by Billy the Bursar, who showers the Great Land-Owner with a precious country-side commodity. Let us hope the honest rustic wakes to share with us more of his Gulli-vants, Fanny-tasies, and his Pimpern-eloquence!

is 1794 cartoon by 18th Century master
phreys, we see mentally-weak King
rge III, often called "Farmer George," as a
rn bore slumped half-insensible across a
, muttering his catch-phrase "What? What?
t? What's the matter now?" Meanwhile,
ting from his ailing mind are the forms of
nal characters such as Gulliver and Fanny
whom the deluded monarch believed to

comprise a secret band protecting him from foreign assault. "Billy the Bursar," simultaneously
eating one of "Mother Threadneedle's Fine
Pies" (a reference to the Bank of England, in
Threadneedle Street) while evacuating gold
coins from his bowels, is George's Prime
Minister William Pitt, then facing criticism for
lavishing funds upon yet another of the King's
ridiculous Royal indulgences.

hmm.

PLENTY TO THINK ABOUT, EH?

AND I MUST SAY, THAT FANNY HILL STUFF WAS A BIT OF ALL RIGHT, TOO.

I DON'T SUPPOSE YOU FANCY...?

tt.

umg?

IT'S ALL RIGHT. IT'S ALL RIGHT, DARLING. GO BACK TO SLEEP.

THAT'S
THANKS,
...M. WE CAN
...A LIFT UP
...TH FROM THIS
...NCTION...

ALLAN?

OVER HERE
WHEN YOU'VE GOT
A MOMENT.

DARLING, THAT'S
THE *FOOTBRIDGE*.

IT TAKES YOU OVER
THE MOTORWAY TO
THE SIDE WITH THE
SOUTH-BOUND
TRAFFIC.

I THOUGHT
WE WERE HEADED
NORTH?

YES.

HOPEFULLY,
SO DOES EVERY-
ONE *ELSE.*

DO TRY AND KEEP
UP, SWEETHEART.

Arrng.

Ong...

JUST HOLD STILL. WE'RE NEARLY THERE.

Oh, Jimmy.

JIMMY, JIMMY, JIMMY.

THEY MADE LOOK A OF A CU HAVEN' THEY, MAN

HALLO, HALLO, HALLO! LOVELY SEEING YOU AGAIN.

JIMMY, THIS IS MISS NIGHT, THAT I WAS TELLING YOU ABOUT.

PLEASED TO MEET YOU.

LIKEWISE.

SIR HUGO YOU KNOW, OF COURSE...

WELL, OF *COURSE* HE BLOODY DOES, A BLOODY FACE LIKE *MINE*.

ONCE SEEN, NEVER BLOODY *FORGOTTEN*, EH?

SCARED THE OUT OF LITTL HERE, FIRST SHE MET M

UNCLE HUGO, I W *FIVE*...

YES. HELPING YOUR DAD, WASN'T I? CLEARING ALL THE KIKES AND COMMIES OUT OF HIS *FACTORIES*...

Hm.

LOOK, WE'D BEST GET DOWN TO BUSINESS.

OF COURSE. SORRY, OLD BOY. YOU KNOW ME. LIVING IN THE PAST.

NOT AT ALL.

COME ON. OUR INTRUDERS CAN'T HAVE GONE FAR.

IN FACT, WE THINK WE HAVE THE CAB-DRIVER WHO FERRIED THEM AWAY LAST NIGHT.

WE'VE GOT HER IN INTERROGATION JUST ALONG HERE...

...HEAR IT AGAIN, ALL RIGHT? AND THIS TIME KEEP YOUR KNEES TOGETHER, YOU LITTLE PRO.

⸮uhuhuhu⸮

O-OH GOD. LOOK, PLEASE, I'VE TOLD YOU EVERYTHING...

I-I DROPPED THEM IN BROOKGATE.

THEY SAID THEY WERE LEAVING TODAY.

TH-THEY SAID THEY WERE HEADING NORTH.

CAR PARK

...TH, THEN. THEY'LL W WE HAVE PUBLIC NSPORT COVERED.

MY GUESS IS THEY'LL HITCH-HIKE.

I MUST SAY, DRUMMOND, YOUR GOD-DAUGHTER'S A SMASHER...

YES. AND JOHNNY NIGHT WAS MY BEST PAL.

YOU TOUCH HER, AND I'LL HAVE YOUR THROAT OUT.

WORD TO THE WISE, EH?

WORD TO THE WISE.

NOW, THEN...

...LET'S FIND THESE FUCKING ANARCHISTS.

MINA, WHY ARE WE HEADED *SOUTH?* WE SAID WE'D MEET OUR COLOURED CHUM AND HIS DUTCH GIRLS IN *SCOTLAND...*

I CHANGED MY MIND.

AFTER ALL, OUR PEOPLE WILL WAIT FOR US.

ALSO, THAT DOSSIER MENTIONED A PUBLIC SCHOOL THAT I KNOW IS IN *KENT...*

KENT? YOU'RE JOKING.

ALLAN, DON'T BE DENSE.

OOH, LOOK! ONE'S STOPPING FOR US.

LOOK LIVEL BRING THE SU DARLING, WO YOU?

HELLO. WE'RE HEADING FOR KENT. IS THAT BEING CHEEKY?

MISSUS, YOU CAN BE AS CHEEKY AS YOU LIKE. I'M HEADING DOWN BRADGATE WAY.

THAT'S JUST WHERE WE'RE GOING.

COME ON, LOVEY. HOP IN.

YOU'LL HAVE TO SIT ON YOUR CHAP'S LAP, DARLIN'. I'M SURE HE WON'T MIND.

THERE. EVERYONE IN ?

I'M NEW, WORKING FOR CALLENDAR, SO MUSTN'T MISS TH DELIVERIES

SURE. WE'RE OODLES AND AL, BY THE WAY.

HOW DO.

I'M ALBERT.

COVERSA MULTIT...

FRAMPTON OVERCOAT

CALLENDARS

GZ7216

BRADGA FIRCOME

LARKIN

HE WAS NICE, WASN'T HE?

WELL, IF YOU LIKE TALLY-BOYS, GETTING PEOPLE INTO *DEBT* FOR A LIVING.

MINA, WHAT ARE WE DOING HERE?

WELL, THERE WERE ALL THESE *JOTTINGS*, IN THE *DOSSIER*.

NOTES FROM GERALD O'BRIEN TO "H.W."...

WAIT A MINUTE... O'BRIEN THE REPLACEMENT *PARTY* LEADER?

THAT'S HIM. "H.W." MUST BE GENERAL SIR HAROLD WHARTON, OR "BIG BROTHER" AS THEY CALLED HIM.

THEY'RE OLD NOTES. WHARTON DIED IN '52.

THERE'S ALSO AN "R.K.C." MENTIONED.

LORD KNOWS WHO *HE* IS, BUT APPARENTLY HE ATTENDED PUBLIC SCHOOL WITH WHARTON, HERE IN BRADGATE.

WHICH SCHOOL'S THAT, THEN?

GREYFRIARS.

LOOKS BOARDED-UP TO ME.

Mm. STILL WORTH A VISIT, I'LL BET.

ALLAN, DO YOU REMEMBER RICHARD HANNAY? WORKED AT MI5 BEFORE THE WAR?

HANNAY? YES. DECENT SORT OF CHAP, I ALWAYS THOUGHT.

ABSOLUTELY. ANYWAY, HANNAY ONCE TOLD ME ABOUT THAT "THIRTY-NINE STEPS" BUSINESS HE INVESTIGATED.

OH, YES. ALL TERRIBLY CRYPTIC, WASN'T IT?

"WHAT ARE THE THIRTY-NINE STEPS?" AND ALL THAT.

YES, WE APPARENTL WALKING THE/

ARE WE?

WHAT, THE ACTUAL THIRTY-NINE STEPS?

THE VERY SAME. DICK HANNAY SAID THEY LED TO THE SECRET AT BRITISH INTELLI- GENCE'S HEART.

FRANKLY, I NEVER UNDERSTOOD WHAT HE MEANT.

ALTHOUGH NOW I THINK I MAY HAVE AN INKLING.

REALLY? SO WHAT'S THIS BIG SECRET, THEN?

I DON'T KNOW.

LET'S FIND OUT, SHALL WE?

Bloody hell.

I HEARD THEY'D CLOSED ALL THE PUBLIC SCHOOLS DURING THE BIG BROTHER YEARS, BUT EVEN *SO...*

...IT'S A BIT OF A SHOCK, SEEING IT ALL LIKE THIS.

WELL, HOPEFULLY IT'LL REVEAL MORE ABOUT OUR FORMER *BOSSES* THAN THEY KNOW ABOUT *US.*

YOU KNOW, YOU REALLY SHOULDN'T HAVE DOZED OFF LAST NIGHT.

WHAT, BECAUSE I MISSED THESE CLUES IN THE DOSSIER?

NO, IDIOT. YOU MISSED *ME.*

GOD, I WAS RANDY AFTER THAT *FANNY HILL* SEQUEL.

Oh.

YES, I READ THAT IN THE CAB, EARLIER...

Mm. I *THOUGHT* YOU HAD, WHEN I WAS ON YOUR KNEE IN ALBERT'S *VAN.*

ha ha.

OH, AM I?

OU U, YOU'RE TY LITTLE GGAR...

WELL, WE'LL FIND DIGS WHEN WE'VE FINISHED HERE. THEN WE'LL SEE.

WHAT ABOUT NOW? THIS DUMP'S OBVIOUSLY DESERTED...

HA! ALL THESE SCHOOLBOY MEMO-RIES GOT YOU GOING, HAVE THEY?

GO ON, THEN. LET'S SEE WHAT...

Er...I-I SAY? A-Are YOU...?

AAAA!

LOCKE

...S A BIT OF A SHEEP, WHARTON. N, YOU KNOW. HT UP BY SOME LY COLONEL.

BORN **LEADER**, THOUGH. OH CRIKEY, YES.

HE GOT MIXED UP WITH **COMMUNISTS**, AN OIK NAMED SKINPOLE FROM **ST. JIMS**.

NEXT THING, HE'S ENLISTED IN THE **ARMY**. GENERAL IN NO TIME.

WAR'S END, HE JOINED THE LABOUR PARTY AND GOT THAT GHASTLY NICKNAME. THE REST YOU KNOW.

THIS IS MY DORM, INCIDENTALLY, THROUGH HERE.

NOT MUCH, I KNOW. STILL, FOR SAYING IT WAS THE NAPPER'S OFFICE, IT'S JOLLY COMFY.

WHEN WHARTON'S LOT CLOSED THIS PLACE DOWN, I EXPECT THEY LET ME STAY ON BECAUSE THEY WERE **SORRY** FOR ME.

I MEAN, IT SAYS **SOMETHING** THAT I DIDN'T END UP IN SOME ROTTEN **CAMP** OR OTHER.

BESSIE'S INFLUENCE, I EXPECT.

BESSIE. KILLED LF THE WEEK WHARTON'S T ATTACK.

UNLESS THE SPIES GOT HER, OF COURSE.

ALWAYS PLENTY OF THEM AROUND GREYFRIARS.

WHAT DO YOU MEAN, SPIES?

OH, GREYFRIARS PRODUCED **ALL** THE CLOAK-AND-DAGGER CHAPS. THEY WERE...

I-I SAY... **YOU'RE** NOT SPIES, ARE YOU?

LET'S SAY WE USED TO BE. NOW WE DON'T LIKE THEM ANY MORE THAN **YOU** DO.

SO, THEY GROOMED SPIES HERE, DID THEY?

OH, YES. EVER SINCE THE *FIRST* GLORIANA WAS QUEEN.

OH, I SAY, THERE'S A PICTURE IN THE *MUSEUM* YOU CAN SEE. IT'S ALONG HERE...

WERE MI5 RECRUITING WHEN YOU STUDIED HERE?

NOT HALF. THAT WAS OLD QUELCHY. HENRY QUELCH.

HE WAS REMOVE MASTER. GIMLET-EYED OLD DEVIL.

HE WAS WATCHING WHARTON FROM THE START, ALONG WITH NIGHT AND CHERRY AND WAVERLY AND THE REST.

HERE ARE. NATL HISTOR MUSEU

THERE. GOOD QUEEN GLORY HERSELF.

1564, I THINK IT WAS, WHEN SHE VISITED GREYFRIARS. NEVER WAS MUCH GOOD AT HIST, I'M AFRAID.

THE RUM-LOOKING FELLOW BEHIND HER SIR JACK WILTON. HE GLORIANA'S BIG CHIE SO I'M TOLD.

YOU KNOW, I'D BET MY SCROG ALLO THAT HE WAS HERE S ING FOR TALENT, EV BACK *THEN*.

WHAT ABOUT THESE OTHER BOYS YOU MENTIONED?

OH, QUELCH DREW THEM ALL IN.

JOHNNY NIGHT, FOR EXAMPLE, HE ENDED UP DESIGNING *BRAIN-WASHING* MACHINES.

SIR JOHN NIGHT, THE INDUSTRIAL-IST?

THAT'S HIM. DIED NOT LONG BACK.

I'D SEE THEM ALL AT THE OLD BOY'S REUNIONS, AND WE'D CHIN-WAG...

JOHNNY...HE'D HAD A FEW... SAID LANDED AN MI5 CONTRACT DESIGN KIT FOR SOME *WELSH* SET-UP.

D-DREAM INDUCERS.

KILLER BALLOONS.

YAROOH, EH?

...OH ...ED.

...ING? I THINK ...W WHO DESIGNED ...N-GUN THAT ...SHOT AT US...

OH, NIGHT INDUSTRIES HANDLED *ALL* THAT ROT.

THEY DID FOR *BRITISH* INTELLIGENCE, AT ANY RATE. AND JOHNNY WAS ALWAYS PRETTY TIGHT WITH *WAVERLY,* AS WELL.

AND WHO WAS THIS WAVERLY?

FRANCIS ALEXANDER WAVERLY. HE RUNS SOME SPY-RING FOR THE UNITED NATIONS THESE DAYS.

LOOK, SHALL WE GO OUTSIDE? THERE'S A REAR DOOR...

...AT'S ...ER.

IT'S PROBABLY MY IMAGINATION, BUT I THOUGHT IT WAS GETTING A BIT *STUFFY* IN HERE.

WE, UH...

WE HADN'T NOTICED.

ANYWAY, WHERE WERE WE?

OH YES, WAVERLY.

NIGHTY LANDED A U.N. CONTRACT THROUGH HIM. SAID THE COUSINS WOULDN'T LIKE IT.

HE MEANT THE *YANKS.*

WHY WOULDN'T THEY LIKE IT?

WELL, I SUPPOSE THEY'D WANT *THEIR* CHAPS TO GET THE BIG CONTRACTS, WOULDN'T THEY?

JOHNNY DIDN'T CARE, THOUGH.

...MPANY ...OLLY ...LL.

QUELCHY'S SON, QUENTIN, WORKED THERE BEFORE HE JOINED MI5'S *TECHNICAL* CHAPPIES.

LIKE *EVERYBODY* THERE, HE'S KNOWN BY AN *INITIAL.*

WELL, AT LEAST EVERYBODY *I* KNOW, LIKE GOOD OLD BOB.

BOB? WHAT INITIAL DID THEY GIVE HIM, THEN?

OH, MIDDLE OF THE ALPHABET. CAN'T HAVE BEEN VERY HIGH IN THE PECKING ORDER.

I THINK BOB WAS "M."

SOMETHING LIKE THAT, ANYWAY.

HOLD ON A MOMENT. WHO WAS BOB, AGAIN?

OH, DIDN'T I SAY? BOB CHERRY. WHARTON'S BEST CHUM IN THE LOWER FOURTH REMOVE.

AWFULLY DECENT CHAP. ALWAYS THE MOST DANGEROUS FELLOW IN ANY GIVEN *SCRAP*, BUT A JOLLY CHEERFUL TYPE, ALL THE SAME.

I REMEMBER HE'D WAKE ME IN THE MORNINGS. "HALLO, HALLO, HALLO, BILLY, YOU FAT SNEAK! RISE AND SHINE!"

HAPPY DAYS, EH?

HE SOUNDS CHARMING.

I DON'T SUPPOSE HIS MIDDLE INITIAL WAS "K," WAS IT?

CRIKEY, YES! ROBERT KIM CHERRY. HOW DID YOU KNOW *THAT*?

HIS FATHER NAMED HIM KIM AFTER THE FAMOUS *SPY* WHO WORKED IN *AFGHANISTAN*.

BOB CERTAINLY LIVED UP TO THE *NAME*.

HOW DO YOU MEAN?

WELL, YOU KNOW. ALL THE HAIR-RAISING LARKS AND SHADY BUSINESS.

COURSE, HIS NAME WASN'T *CHERRY* DURING ALL *THAT*.

OH? WHAT W[A]S IT?

UM....SOME *OTHER* SORT OF FRUIT, I THINK. WAS IT "LEMON" OR SOMETHING?

OH GOD. LIME.

"R.K.C." IS HARRY *LIME*.

OH, I SAY! YOU CHAPS HAVE CERTAINLY DONE YOUR *PREP*.

YOU *KNOW* HIM, THEN?

RATHER TOO WELL. WE THINK HE'S CURRENTLY PURSUING US.

PEESE

OH, ROTTEN LUCK.

WHENEVER HE PURSUED *ME* HE GENERALLY *CAUGHT* ME, YOU KNOW.

YOU'LL BE LUCKY NOT TO GET A BOOTING, IN MY EXPERIENCE.

...Mm. OR A
...OOTING, IN *MY*
...XPERIENCE.

WILLIAM,
WE'RE TREMENDOUS-
LY GRATEFUL. YOU'VE
BEEN VERY, VERY
HELPFUL TO US.

HASN'T HE,
DARLING?

YES, I
SUPPOSE
HE HAS.

SO PRACTICALLY
EVERY MAJOR BRITISH
SPY CAME FROM THIS
PLACE, EH?

YES. WE'RE
NOT TERRIBLY
FAMOUS, BUT
WE'RE
INFLUENTIAL.

IT'S THE OLD SCHOOL
MOTTO, I EXPECT.
*"Conamur Tenues
Grandia."*

*"THOUGH
SLIGHT, WE
STRIVE FOR
GREATNESS."*

YES. YES,
APPARENTLY
YOU'VE STRIVED
LIKE MAD.

ANYWAY, I WANT YOU
TO HAVE THIS FIFTY POUNDS.
THAT SHOULD KEEP YOU
IN BUNS.

GOSH! THANKS
AWFULLY! I'VE NEVER
SEEN SO MUCH
RHINO!

YOU *DO* SEEM
RATHER HARD-UP. HOW
DO YOU GET *BY,* LIVING
ALONE HERE?

W-WELL, I STILL
GET POSTAL ORDERS
FROM MOTHER,
OCCASIONALLY.

B-BUT WHAT ABOUT
YOU FELLOWS? SHALL
YOU BE ALL RIGHT?
CHERRY CAN GET
PRETTY *WAXY...*

THANKS FOR
THE CONCERN,
BUT WE'LL BE
DANDY.

WE'LL TAKE AN EVASIVE
ROUTE NORTH FROM HERE.
PERHAPS VISIT THE BIRMING-
HAM SPACEPORT. MI5 WON'T
CATCH US.

THANKS AGAIN
FOR YOUR HELP,
WILLIAM.

OH, I
SAY, NOT
AT ALL.

BEST OF LUCK,
YOU CHAPS, EH? DON'T
END UP GETTING SENT
TO PUNNY. CHEERIO.

CHEERIO.

YOU'RE AWFULLY QUIET. PENNY FOR THEM.

Hm?

OH, I WAS THINKING ABOUT THAT *SPACEPORT*. ARE YOU REALLY PLANNING ON PAYING IT A VISIT?

WELL, I DON'T SEE WHY *NOT*.

SPACE SCIENCE HAS OBVIOUSLY PROGRESSED, THIS LAST DECADE.

IT COULDN'T HURT TO FIND OUT ABOUT IT.

NO, YOU'RE RIGHT. AND I QUITE FANCY SEEING A SPACEPORT. FRANKLY, EVEN AIRPORTS ARE STILL A NOVELTY.

THAT'S SETTLED BIRMIN IT IS.

IN THE MEANTIME, LET'S GET SOME FISH AND CHIPS AND SHOP FOR SEASIDE POSTCARDS.

THEN WE'LL FIND A GUEST-HOUSE.

SOMEWHERE WHERE WE'RE ALONE.

MUMS PLAICE

WILLIAM BROWN CAPTURED

OUTLAWS

Ohhhhhhh.

GOD, I NEEDED THAT.

WHAT, THE FISH AND CHIPS? GOD, YES. I WAS ABSOLUTELY *FAMISHED.*

Hahaha.

SWINE. COME HERE AND GIVE US A KISS.

Nnm.

Mmm. HERE, YOU DON'T WANT TO BE A LOVE AND GET ME THAT DOSSIER, DO YOU?

HUH. WHAT DID YOUR LAST SERVANT DIE OF?

...LLOPING ...*PISM,* IF ...MEMBER ...RECTLY.

...OME ON, ...E IT HERE. I ...NT TO READ ...OME MORE.

YES, ALL RIGHT. KEEP YOUR SHIRT ON.

WELL, THAT'S NOT WHAT YOU WERE SAYING TWENTY MINUTES AGO.

NOW, WHERE HAD I GOT TO?

IT WAS JUST AFTER THE 18th CENTURY STUFF...

HERE WE ARE....oh.

HERE, DARLING, LOOK AT THIS.

IT'S *US.*

SHADOWS IN THE STEAM

Being a True and Faithful
Mappe of Ye Blazing Worlde
— in its several partes —

IRON MOUNTAINS

NORTH POLE

ATLANTIC OCEAN

EMMANUEL COLLEGE CAMBRIDGE

See now the symmetry of God's design,
With iron mountains ringed about each Pole,
And next fantastic archipelagos,
With Magapatagonia in the South
And here the Blazing Worlde, both ruled by beasts
That have the tongue and semblance yet of men.
I came hereby, with sprites of Earth and Aire,
And one call'd Christian, not of this worlde made,
And saw its alabaster wharfs and quays;
Its visions of vermillion and jade.
Good Trav'ller, know this place is
    rightly feared,
            Fit only for the dead, or disappeared.

Here, by the testament of Captain Clegg, is
found the Streaming Kingdoms, wherein
transformed spirits of drowned mariners are
ruled by an intelligence called only 'His
Imperial Wetness'. It may be this realm is of
a kind with that of the much talked of
'water-babes.' — L.G.

The Radiance in these climes is of two partes,
One Red like Mars, the other Venus–green,
With variously glass'd pince-nez required
    comprised of ruby and of emrald both.
Thus furnished, we may fill our eyes and ears
    With lights and musics come from
            higher spheres.

1666   1695

XXIII
XIII

SHADOWS IN THE STEAM

1898, AND THE GENESIS OF THE
MARK I MURRAY GROUP

FROM

MEMOIRS OF AN ENGLISH INTELLIGENCER

BY

CAMPION BOND

H.W.—
Managed to save a copy of this from Litpol's
furnaces. It's of special interest, as R.K.C. tells me
that Murray herself may still be alive, albeit as
some hideous old relic in her eighties by now.
Best to you and Bessie (the real "B.B.", eh?)
yours, G.O'B.

MEESONS AND CO. LIMITED
ST. MARTIN'S STREET, LONDON
1908

IT WAS DURING the late months of 1897 that I was required to visit the impressively (and also, to my way of thi
startlingly) appointed offices of England's Military Intelligence command at Vauxhall Cross, where I was welc
by the serving head of operations, universally acclaimed professor of mathematics, the esteemed James Moriarty
deceased. A well-liked, lively-minded gentleman of middle years, he always had what seemed a merry twinkle
eye, even whilst in discussions of great gravity or moment, and in this regard the instance of my visit would pro
exception. Sitting there across the generous expanse of his broad, handsome desk from me, he smiled and gesture
engagingly, his pale, delicate hands in almost constant motion as he outlined for me what he thought, with his
master's foresight, would be the unprecedented challenges to Great Britain's security during the twentieth ce
which at that time seemed to be looming somewhat ominously, not so very far ahead.

The way that 'M' (as we referred to the professor) saw things, unknown and potentially apocalyptic dangers
within the breathtaking advances made by science itself, along with the appearance of a new and ruthless breed o
who would not hesitate to take advantage of such new discoveries despite, or even possibly because of, their ala
nature. As evidence of this new savage strain of science-brigand, Moriarty cited the example of the Hunnish
Piraten," Captain Mors, along with that of his French rival, the repulsive Monsieur Robur.

Yet it was not in the realm of the known sciences alone that the professor felt our hydra-headed threat was
ing. He believed, perhaps eccentrically, that Britain might prove subject to hostilities emerging from the area most
monly regarded as the haunted terrain of the supernatural. I must stress here that the professor, putting his more
manifested megalomania for a moment to one side, was a fierce rationalist and firm materialist, intensely logica
his ways. Thus he regarded the occurrence of peculiar phenomena not as an evidence of supernature, but, more
erly, as evidence of nature incompletely comprehended.

Perhaps adhering to the ancient (and, if but considered for a moment, dangerously misguided) dictum that e:
us to fight fire with fire, it was to this end that 'M' ventured his proposal, which suggested an assembly, in the m
of a team or squadron, of unusually gifted or experienced individuals working clandestinely for the Crown, by
means England might successfully repel and counter such incursions from the unknown as it seemed that the pro
now daily anticipated. His idea was not, he put it to me, wholly without precedent, and indicated to me a stout
dusty folders that had up until that moment gone unnoticed, heaped upon a distant corner of Professor Moriarty's
Perusing these antique and badly faded documents, I learned that such a cabinet of human oddities was first com
by England's first head of intelligence, the legendary Sir Jack Wilton, early in the reign of England's so-called
monarch" Gloriana in the sixteenth century. Further to this, it seemed that during the ill-starred reign of King G
the Third the scheme was resurrected with a fresh ensemble of unlikely and outlandish characters to fill the vaca
left by the former members of the group, long since departed.

When I asked where we were to discover latter-day equivalents of the unusual personalities comprising thes
earlier assemblages, 'M' merely smiled and gestured, calling my attention to a single folder, far less tattered a
clearly a more recent vintage than its fellows. Opening it to peer within I found it to contain a small selection of
paper articles and brief appended notes, mostly pertaining to events that had occurred within the previous ten ye
so. It gradually dawned upon me that these various reports concerned the actions of just five specific individuals

One set of documents pertained to the purchase of heliotropes, imported from the remote nation of Bengod
student at the London University, while supplementing these receipts were newspaper accounts of an "invisible
strosity" which, several commentators speculated, might have some connection to the probably-invented "horla"
ture that the French claimed to have captured in the later 1880s. Other papers had circled obituaries: an explore
had been reported killed in some lost kingdom far away in Africa; a fiendishly inventive Indian mutineer believ
have been drowned almost a quarter-century before; also, a medical practitioner from Edinburgh transplanted do
London and apparently become a suicide in 1886. Added to these were files relating to the recent scandalous di
of a young lady music teacher by the name of Harker, clipped to which there were bewildering appended notes
ring to unpleasant graveyard desecrations up in the vicinity of Highgate Cemetery, with decapitated corpses ar
like in evidence.

It was to these last writings that Professor Moriarty now drew my attention. He explained to me the scarcely
ible events in which our Mrs. Harker (who, reverting to her maiden name immediately after her divorce, now
herself Miss Wilhelmina Murray) had become embroiled at the beginnings of the current year. As the professo
things, this young woman had survived, both physically and mentally, an onslaught instigated by a prime mature
from a species of which we had hitherto refuted the existence. In addition, she possessed invaluable and almos
tainly unique experience concerning the direct effect of so-called supernatural phenomena at first hand, and wi
divorce had demonstrated, at least in the eyes of the professor, a determined spirit that he thought might qualify
the head of his proposed team. I protested that, entirely to the contrary, her very gender had disqualified her from
sideration as a seriously-regarded leader, at which the professor glanced with much significance towards a portr
Her Majesty that hung adorning his far office wall. He stated his belief that wilful, self-directed men such as tho
proposed should make up the remainder of this curious league would not feel the same territorial rivalry towa
woman as they would invariably feel, confronted by a male commander. Whilst at the time I will admit to a belie
the professor's theories were outlandish and unnecessarily progressive, I must equally concede that over tim
insights proved to be correct in almost every measure.

Further to the matter of Miss Murray, he observed that after her alleged violation by a creature that was less
human and her subsequent divorce from the estate agent who'd previously been her husband, she would surely
herself in a precarious and vulnerable position, by virtue of her newly found pariah status as both ruined woman
willing divorcee. Ostracised by polite society on these accounts, it seemed, then, a foregone conclusion that our
teacher would quite shortly come to be in a condition of considerable monetary hardship, which, so the professo
soned, might make her unusually susceptible to our proposal of a lucrative, albeit rather hazardous mode of em
ment. He suggested that I first recruit this woman (who had currently, by all accounts, found rented roor

ndsey), and next enlist her to locate and hire the other persons that 'M' wished to see included in his nightmar-
emble.

ffice it to say that by the following day I had made postal contact with our quarry, guardedly making ambiguous
s as to the possibility of subsequent employ. Meeting with an enthusiastic, even slightly desperate response by
n of post, I had arranged to meet with her beside the lake there in St. James's Park. Arriving early for our assig-
I was earnestly engaged in throwing breadcrumbs to the ducks when a polite cough by my shoulder gave me
o turn.

e first thing to impress itself upon me was the slightness of her build, and her diminutive appearance, standing
ore than five feet tall. It seemed to me that a strong wind might snap her in two at the waist, let alone the more
us and actively aggressive forces that Professor Moriarty had it in his labyrinthine mind for her to meet with.
noticed the tight-wound suggestion of repression and restraint she seemed to carry with her, an impression of
urious resentment that she kept withheld beneath her perfectly-composed exterior. As if to emphasise this,
. the day was by no means a cold one, she wore tightly wrapped about her throat a long red scarf with which she
elf-consciously throughout our interview, her eyes filled with darting suspicion and uncertainty, her lips pursed
t seemed a moue of almost constant disapproval or distaste.

r discussions by the waterside, with trees made dark inverted masses of viridian reflected in the lake before us,
oth brief and to the point. Though she seemed mistrustful of me from the start until the finish of our conversa-
nce I had remarked on the impressive sum her reimbursements would amount to, and assured her there should
mmorality in her employ, she readily agreed and asked me what should be her first assignment. I explained that
ployer, Mr. 'M', would presently arrange for her to be transported in a British naval vessel to the waters west of
America. There she'd be put down in a boat and left to make her own way to the enigmatic Lincoln Island, where
her task to enlist the reputedly-dead Indian Mutineer turned science-rogue that I had read of in Professor
ty's notes.

musingly, Miss Murray (as she constantly insisted she be called), believing herself to be both well read and
l, had seemingly assumed, from various pointed remarks she made, that 'M' was Mr. Mycroft Holmes, who
succeed Professor Moriarty as head of intelligence. I did not, it must be said, seek at the time to rectify her quite
ous conclusions. Rather, I informed her that, anticipating her agreement to our princely offer, we had opened an
it for her at Lloyd's, and had secreted in advance her first month's wage. This was upon the understanding that
uld report to Government-maintained docks close to Wapping at her earliest convenience, where she would next
ence her journey to the South Pacific.

ll this was settled without disagreement, and some eight days later our absurdly tiny suffragettist music-teacher
n route for South America and, hopefully, for Lincoln Island with its brilliant, dangerous Sikh inhabitant.
ding to the naval officers accompanying Miss Murray on this first leg of her journey, she kept to her cabin for
p's duration, studying the files pertaining to the Indian privateer that we'd provided, this despite some several
ions to dine at the captain's table, her refusal earning her the soubriquet of 'Iron Drawers' amongst the lower
At length, when it had been decided that the ship was now but some short distance to the south-east of the island
as its objective, Murray was set down within a lifeboat that contained provisions more than adequate for the brief
f rowing that would take her to the shores of Lincoln. Unexpectedly, however, Murray's craft had not gone more
n lengths from our naval steamer when it was enveloped in a dense fog that had seemingly swelled up from
re. Some years later, we discovered that these permanent great banks of mist conceal the group of islands called
allaro Archipelago, but at the time of Miss Murray's adventure, lacking all such information, we were unprepared
us lost contact with her scarcely moments after setting her adrift. An hour later violent storms arose and, fearing
rst, our ship set sail for Blighty, leaving our poor music-instructress for dead. The following entries, then, col-
rom Miss Murray's journal notes, are our sole record of what next transpired.

t is now some few days since I was parted from the ship, and yet this is the first occasion I have had to make a
count within this journal. Briefly, then, I was set down within my rowboat on the ship's port side, at night, almost
k ago exactly from today. I was at the time experiencing some relief to find the waters nowhere near as rough as
previously anticipated, and was to a small extent congratulating myself on how jolly brave and capable I had
out to be, despite my wholesale lack of any previous experience with this kind of high jinks. It was at this point
e ship behind me, along with the waters that surrounded me and stars above, completely vanished, swallowed in
tant by a dense white fog that all but instantly reduced me to an abject and despicable example of the most utter-
less whimpering femininity, with no idea of which way she was headed or of where she was, save that she was
probably in the most awful trouble. This fact was confirmed, with what seemed an unnecessarily harsh emphasis,
s a half-hour later, when a wind began to rise that was attended by some of the largest waves that I have ever
et alone been adrift by night amongst.

am not wholly certain as to in quite what order the events that next transpired occurred, since I was, you may
ne, in a state of dreadful panic at the time. I was huddled, at some point, there at the bottom of my lifeboat, cling-
the waterproof trunk which contained all my provisions (with this journal in amongst them), unable to hear my
rantic screaming for the anvil waves that smashed and crashed about me. All at once, amidst my terror, I felt in
omach a most frightful sense of bottomlessness that I knew must mean my fragile craft had been raised high aloft
ome towering wave, where it now hung for but a second before dropping through the air to land inverted in a
ing foam of white and midnight green.

have a memory of being underwater with no clear sense of where 'up' might be, and feel I may have rather bashed
ead upon my boat's disintegrating timbers, but at any rate it seems that I did not release my hold upon the trunk,
, being watertight, presumably at last bobbed to the surface, acting as a kind of buoy. It was to this I found myself
inging when I woke, my cheek pressed in a reach of pale blonde sand spread between knuckles of obsidian rock,
at I hoped to be the shores of Lincoln Isle. It was first light, the eastern heavens now a nacreous grey as I climbed

to my feet unsteadily and looked about me in the pre-dawn twilight. At my back the surf retreated, hissing, leav
crabs of brilliant green stranded in sinks and pools amongst dark granite crags. Before me, the fine talcum of th
rose at a gentle incline to its crest, a spinal ridge where tufts of maram-grass made a fine hatching, penned in jet
the lightening sky.

"The various layers of formal clothing I had been impractical enough to dress myself in were now soak
thus become intolerably heavy. Since the morning did not seem by any means a cold one, having dragged my tru
further up the sands to safety from the frothing tidal edge, I next removed my garb down to my modest unde
and spread the sloughed-off coats and skirts like black and saturated banners on the rough-cut stony outcrops
my intention to eat first from my provisions, safe within the trunk, and possibly compose some plan of action
waited for my garments to be dried by the soon-risen sun, but this was not to be. As I sat on a somewhat highe
perch, plucking my damp chemise away from goose-bumped skin and looking, I suppose, to all the world lik
American advertisement for soap, I was surprised by what seemed like a great and silent tidal surge of men, sl
forms that welled up of a sudden from the gloaming to engulf my lofty spar and wash me quite away upon a cu
strong arms, my sopping crimson scarf trailed out behind me in the wake, cry stifled by a leathery hand that s
of rope and tar across my mouth.

"When my assailants had delivered me once more to level ground I was set down, at which a low voic
beside my ear cautioned me three times not to scream again, this admonition not only enunciated in clear Engl
likewise in German and in French. Having nodded in compliance, the firm grip across my mouth was next relea:
I was able thus to turn my head and take the measure of my captors stood about me there, their features being
moment more discernible, both from the gradually improving light and from my eyes having become accusto
the gloom. They were a motley, roughneck crew some five or six in number, and amidst even so small a sample
evident that these men hailed from a variety of continents and likewise were the issue of some several differen
One, I think, was a Malay, another being a tall Negro with the elegant bone-structure and near-indigo complexi
I most associate with Africa's Ivory Coast. There was an older man that I assumed to be American whose voic
New England twang about it, and a fellow similarly aged, dressed up in what appeared to be an ancient, threadba
form such as were common during the Sepoy Rebellion.

"The man who'd spoken and whose hand had gagged me was, as it turned out, a young and rather we
Englishman whose name, I later learned, was Jack. This last stood barefoot there upon the glistening, tide-sm
sands, nude to his waist so that between his shoulder-blades I could make out in broad tattoo an arrow that I too
a mark of former penal servitude, perhaps implying him to be a transportee escaped whilst bound for New Soutł
or some such ghastly destination. Having first established I was English, he proceeded to interrogate me as to b
name and to the nature of my business there on Lincoln Island, which at least confirmed to me, were confirmatio
ed, that I had indeed arrived at my intended destination.

"Thinking honesty to be upon consideration the best policy, I gave them my full name and told them tha
been paid to come here by British Intelligence in order to convey their highly generous offer to the personage v
assumed was owner of this island, one Prince Dakkar, Indian nobleman turned technologic buccaneer.

"At this their narrow-eyed suspicion turned upon the instant into raucous, ridiculing laughter, and the tattoo
who was my chief interrogator struggled to contain his mirth as he assured me that he knew of no-one here wł
had been called by such a name, putting much stress on the two syllables of 'no-one' as he did so, to renewed ɛ
ment from his colleagues. He then asked me if this was the only name I had been given by the British agents w
sent me here. Had they not given me some other name, he asked, perhaps one more immediately recognisable, by
the Indian prince I sought was known? When my only reply was to shake my head in bewilderment, the compar
more erupted with hilarity, and only the New Englander who looked to be the oldest of the crew seemed ger
indignant upon my behalf. His features crumpled in a disapproving scowl, he muttered that he thought it shamef
these men of government would send a mere girl to approach one they dare not approach themselves, and, wor
this, did not even see fit to tell her the most common name of he she sought, no doubt for fear that she would
terror from their enterprise should she be so informed. My momentary displeasure at his calling me a 'mere gi
immediately displaced by the deep, stomach-churning resonance, as from a gong of dire foreboding that rang t
me. Had I been, so to speak, kept in the dark, upon a mission that already seemed to me quite hazardous enoug
cerning its true dangers?

"I asked them, trying with some difficulty to subdue the tremor in my voice, who, then, it was, if not Prince I
that resided here? The tattooed individual merely shook his head, repeating the word 'no-one,' and commandec
walk ahead of them as they escorted me to see their captain. I protested that I was not dressed, and could not lea
trunk and clothing here within the tide's reach unattended, at which the New Englander took off his trailing oilsk
and let me wear it draped about my shoulders. He instructed the Malay to bring my sodden clothing, and the
Sepoy to retrieve my trunk, and thereupon they marched me up the shore's soft incline, headed for the isle's int

"We walked in silence for perhaps some twenty or so minutes and in all that time saw not another living sou
for an incident near the beginning when we were scarcely past the beach's edge, about to venture into the low,
cropped grass reaching off beyond: a kind of cottage built from bluish-white stones stood there at the sandbar's
margin, and within the darkness of its wooden doorframe I could see a lovely Indian woman in a kind of turquois
or wrapping, standing watching us. She was perhaps some thirty or so years of age, her smouldering umber beau
partly hidden by the air of melancholy hung across her features like a veil. She stared across the sand and grass tu
us from the shadows of her doorway, and the small child she held swaddled in her arms stared also, a pretty
ringleted girl of but a few years old, who had the biggest, brownest and most knowing eyes that I have ever seen.
learned that these two were the estranged wife and daughter of the man I had been sent to find, but at the time sa
the suspicion and resentment in the woman's gaze: the keen intelligence that glowed within the child's. My capt
not give me leave to ask about the pair, but with a gentle push propelled me on across flat scrubland, making

TOP LEFT: Professor James Moriarty, (or 'M'), officiating at Vauxhall Cross. TOP RIGHT: Captain Kettle watches Miss Murray commencing her adventure. BELOW: The rebuilt Nautilus, in dock on Lincoln Island.

threads of wood-smoke twisting up from what I took to be a camp or colony upon the lower flank of purpled,
hills that seemed the island's only landmark.

"The shanty-town, for so it proved to be when finally we reached it, was both more extensive and well-bu
I'd anticipated, with its buildings rising up the hillside's gentle slope in ladder-accessed terraces, and graceful (al
sturdy) walkways of bamboo and hawser strung between them. This novel settlement was also not by any me
mean or bleak as I'd imagined, with instead bright colour and outlandish decorations everywhere, both on its
fronts and upon its population. These I estimated to be several dozen persons of almost as many nationalities, of
men comprised by far the greater part, although they numbered many women and some children in amongst thei
besides. I noticed some men walking hand in hand, both with each other or with younger boys, and so con
Lincoln Isle to be a province founded upon anarchistic principles, providing haven for the deviants…be they p
or sexual by inclination…of the world and all its countries, in a type of libertine utopia, such as was exampled t
Royal in the Caribbean and its many kindred pirate sanctuaries, during earlier centuries.

"At length, walked up a winding path towards the low hill's uppermost extremities, I was brought to a temp
construction, all of stone, that seemed almost a sumptuous palace in compare with the by-no-means meagre str
spread below it upon the inferior slopes of this mauve tumulus. Wide gates of burnished brass opened upon the
of a courtyard flagged with basalt, around which was statuary arranged depicting Hindu deities, plundered perhap
many different sources. I waited under guard within this yard beneath the cold, accusing frowns of octopus-limb
exotic gods while the New Englander ventured alone into the residence itself, after some moments reappearing to
me in.

"I stepped into what seemed a dazzling, regal chamber hung with splendid tapestries, where at the centre, on
ed throne whose back was an exquisitely embroidered peacock tail, sat a tall, turbaned figure of the most alarmi
ferocious aspect, clad in a long coat of such elaborate finery that it appeared at least the jacket of an Admiral, v
epaulettes and decorative frogging, but in bottle green as rich and fraught with both enigma and romance as th
ocean deep itself.

"My New Englander escort having now withdrawn I stood alone there in the silence of that opulent pa
beneath the hawklike and unblinking gaze of that disarming eminence. At last, unable to bear any more of the
ken hush, I spoke, and asked him if he was Prince Dakkar. At this, I thought he almost smiled, but seeing that h
remained as cold and as indifferent, I concluded it to be some aberration of the light. When he replied it was in
less English almost too precise in its enunciation, only faintly accented, his voice deep as the creak in salt-cake
bers. 'Perhaps I was once, but not now. Now I am no-one.' Here he paused for but a single beat and stared unne
ly into my eyes before he went on. 'I am Nemo.'

"The impact of his name upon me was not unlike that of a steam locomotive. I am sure that all the colour d
immediately from my face as finally I understood the constant harping upon 'no-one,' and the Latinate equivale
was implied. The figure sitting here before me, his ring-heavy mocha-coloured fingers toying with his greying
was Captain Nemo. Nemo, the tall, imposing, dusky enemy of all western society, who'd waged a war of terror
high seas and appalled the civilised world at his potent mix of the most up-to-date and modern science or engin
with a bloodily-expressed fanaticism that was all but medieval. Nemo, whose alarming likeness had appeared in
papers and broadsheets all across the length and breadth of Europe, frightening children and their seniors alike
reported death sometime during the middle eighteen seventies, a year or two before I had been even born. I can re
ber, as a baby playing near my mother's skirts, hearing my father and my grandfather debating as to whom ha
the inspiration for more nightmares, Nemo or Napoleon, and now I stood before the man himself, become once
a trembling, stammering infant, scarcely able to believe that my employers had, quite knowingly, sent me unwit
approach this England-hating monster in his den. Did they consider me so casually expendable that they woul
me, careless, to my certain death? Or did they reason me to be equipped uniquely in surviving this encounter, I
earlier this present year lived through the onslaught of a fabulous antagonist more dreadful even than the glov
Sikh?

"Clinging to this last notion and its implication that I was a valued agent in whom my superiors held the h
confidence, I started, hesitatingly, to outline the proposal which I had been sent to put before the captain. Realisin
essentially this was an offer of employment from a nation and a government that Captain Nemo famously desp
thought to take on a more diplomatic tone and couch the bald entreaty in terms more respectful (if not actually
quious) to this evidently proud and isolated self-determined man. I told him that I came to Lincoln Island as the
sary of a British Empire that had lately come to understand the grievous error of their enmity towards the captai
now realized it was his genius alone that could assist them in their hour of need and so enlisted me to venture he
beg him, on my bended knees if necessary, to enlist with them and to accept their reparations, namely a full parde
a handsome reimbursement, along with the promise of adventures extraordinary, here on the coming twentieth
ry's brink.

"This last assurance was my own invention, tendered somewhat desperately as I noticed from the way the ca
brow had clouded that the British Empire's purse or pardon interested him not even slightly. Hoping that I'd judg
personality correctly, which is to say as one with overweening pride as its main principle, I dropped my gaze t
the floor and made apology for having ventured childish imprecations to adventure when I should have understo
such suggestions were, by virtue of the captain's venerable age, entirely inappropriate. I said that I was sorry t
thus intruded upon his retirement here and offered to remove myself forthwith if only there might be a simple ro
found for me, my own having been smashed to driftwood by the recent squall. When these words met with no res
save silence and that same unwavering gaze, I hung my head and turned towards the chamber's tile-rimmed do
I had entered by, making as if to walk away and thinking that my ploy had failed, when suddenly, behind me,
spoke.

"He told me that, to him, the Empire's offers of forgiveness and of money were both deathly insults which

of a different humour, would ensure that my remains were being feasted on by fish before the sun had set that
owever, he went on, he had been pining lately for the exploits that were his in former times, with only a disas-
ircumnavigation of Antarctica attempted three years previously to relieve the cosseted monotony of his listless
here upon Lincoln Isle. He told me to go with his crew, who waited outside in the courtyard still, and that they
find quarters for me where I might rest overnight while he gave my proposal due consideration. He also made
ic note of my attire, with oilskin coat worn over only underwear, suggesting I might try the local woman's wrap,
he referred to as, I think, a 'sa-ree,' until my own clothing could be laundered properly and then returned to me.
ed him for his generosity and did as he'd suggested, though I will confess I passed a nearly sleepless night there
pirate stronghold, much of it spent in a vain attempt to wrap my borrowed tangerine-and-emerald skirts correct-

ie next morning, having had my own attire replaced outside my cabin's door just when I finally appeared to have
-ree' mastered, I was breakfasted alone upon a kedgeree of wood-smoked fish and rice, then taken by the arrow-
d man to meet the captain in a kind of cove there on the island's north-most shore, from which deep, dripping
ored down into the rocky earth and buried waterways below. Attended by some thirty members of the Indian
e-pirate's crew, who carried torches and, I thought, seemed almost bursting with a school-boyish excitement they
scarce conceal, we went into these caverns and down winding passageways made slippery by moss or algae, com-
ally upon a massive, yawning vault whose ceiling, high above, the flickering radiance of the crewmen's fire-
did not touch. Contained within this stygian and echoing expanse there was a night-black subterranean lake, per-
furlong wide, while there upon its waters floated an enormity so utterly unprecedented that even the tide-weath-
ariners surrounding me, familiar with this spectacle, seemed breath-taken to see it now.
There on the lake's jet mirror was the Nautilus, the captain's legendary submersible device, though not, I was
d, the same craft that had terrorized our planet's waterways in Nemo's heyday, this having been sunken some
s before, replaced by the remarkable machine that, in its underground dock, hung suspended there before us now.
test vessel seemed more like some new, unearthly creature than it did a mere insensate mechanism, or perhaps
instead two undersea leviathans, a kraken and a whale, locked in an embrace that was mortal or else amorous.
along a swaying gangway and aboard, the captain thought to tell me that he had decided to accept my offer, and
e were bound for England. He also, in a matter-of-fact way, informed me that if this should prove to be some
h ruse I would immediately be put to death and all of Britain's coastal installations would be levelled by bom-
ent. I was then escorted to a pleasantly-appointed cabin in the submarine's unusually-embellished innards, where
d my watertight trunk and therefore this journal waiting for me. We put out to sea an hour ago, and I am present-
sat within my bunkroom, making these extensive entries and anticipating my return to England, along with the
pointed questions I shall have for the superiors who sent me, unprepared, upon so perilous a quest."
ended Murray's narrative, and I must with regret report that when we met next upon her return to these shores
deed regaled me bitterly with her presumptuous questions and hysterically-delivered accusations, which, attribut-
- outburst to some female difficulty or perhaps an inflammation of the womb, I generously ignored. She'd come
alone to make report upon her jaunt, while the suspicious Captain Nemo and his fascinating craft remained sub-
d at some unknown location, waiting cautiously to see what happened next. So it was that I did not see the cap-
the flesh until the next occasion when I met Miss Murray, being some weeks later at the then still-uncompleted
l causeway, jutting proudly and preposterously out from Dover and into the iron-grey waters of the English
el.
explained her next assignment to her, the retrieval of another superannuated and presumed-dead legend, and
d the sniping and superior tone that had, it seemed, become her custom to use whilst addressing me, along with
ive, misguided speculations as to the identity of 'M,' our ultimate employer. Walking down with her across the
and ladders to the ocean's edge, I was perhaps taken somewhat aback to notice that a frightful churning had
enced there in the ferrous waters not so very far beneath us, as if some great unruly serpent of the depths were
ng amidst the boiling froth and spume. It was, of course, the captain's monstrous underwater battleship, which,
I had by then seen it described in Murray's notes, I was by no means quite prepared for in its awesome actual-
netal gangplank was extended for Miss Murray to repair aboard, and once she'd done so there was a brief, chill-
oment when another, larger figure next appeared there at the aperture by which she'd entered, staring out direct-
ie from beneath the dark briar-hedges of his brows with eyes full of a wintry, sere contempt that I remember with
der to this day. This, then, was Nemo, the most deadly and notorious scientific villain that the nineteenth centu-
spawned. He briefly held my gaze, then with a sneer slammed shut the hatchway, thus allowing his unfathomable
to once more submerge. In only a few moments every trace of it was gone and I was left to stare in stupefac-
the circling, screaming gulls and foam-laced breakers that remained.
s it eventually transpired, Miss Murray and the captain were amongst the least alarming presences that came to
luded in Professor Moriarty's league of curiosities, and I must question now, as then, his wisdom in assembling
ourage of such unbalanced, dangerous individuals. It seems to me the British Empire has always encountered dif-
in distinguishing between its heroes and its monsters, and if the professor had not some ten years ago been taken
lonely, stratospheric grave, I cannot help but feel that he himself might, albeit reluctantly, concur with my assess-
My own ruinous association with the team, extending although tenuously to the present day, has been to the great
ent of my career and is, I have concluded, the main factor which contributes to my current desk job in the files
ment, that I shall discuss in detail and at length in my next chapter.
or now, let it suffice to say that one should never suffer to command a host of nightmares, lest they shrug your
nd turn upon you in your sleep. The coming years, I hope, will not be blighted by such rude awakenings, but, as
ve shall see.

MOBILES IN MOBILE

TRANSLATION: MOBILE
WITHIN A MOBILE ELEMENT

NAUTILUS I, 1865

NAUTILUS II, 1878

ORT

HELM

HATCH

MECHANICAL TENTACLES
4 STARBOARD, 4 PORT

BLOW
HOLE

FORWARD
ESCAPE
HATCH

LIBRARY

NEMO'S
CABIN

LANTERN

AIR
TANK

FRESH
WATER

VIEW
PORT

BRIG

FORWARD
CREW
QUARTERS

STORES

SALON

RWARD
ROPLANE

NAUTILUS II
SEPARATING KRAKEN SECTION
FROM WHALE HULL

PRINCE DAKKAR, 1864

N
W　E
S

5

THE THAMES

6

8

7

10

Here be South
Londoners

KEY

1) THE CAVOR MONUMENT

Erected in St. James Park, London's
st recent statue commemorates the late eccentric
onary Selwyn Cavor, driving force behind 1901's lunar
edition and the subsequent annexation of the moon as
t of the British Empire.

HORNBLOWER'S COLUMN

hough rendered almost unrecognisable by pigeon-
ppings, the statue of Napoleonic naval hero Horatio
nblower atop its tall column in Trafalgar Square remains
e of the capital's best-known and best loved landmarks.

THE DIOGENES CLUB

ough increasingly seen as an anachronism in our new
tury, this staid and exclusive gentlemen's club is still
ular, with a surprising number of Prime Ministers and
inet members frequently popping in for a chat.

THE BRITISH MUSEUM

s institution incited controversy during 1900 when
vspapers spread rumours of a secret 'locked wing'
using fantastical exhibits and tended by equally
robable caretakers. Denials were issued, although
uests to investigate the wing were refused.

WAPPING DOCKS

merly a harbour for Captain Nemo's *Nautilus,* an
curate floating plywood replica of the science-pirate's
mersible boat has been assembled, with a blackface
or impersonating the Captain, greatly boosting the
t End's tourist trade.

6) ROTHERHITHE TUNNEL

Intended to replace Rotherhithe Bridge, destroyed
during 1898, work on the tunnel has been impeded by the
discovery of airship wreckage of Oriental design, and a
distressing number of drowned workers or crewmen, all
Chinese.

7) LIMEHOUSE

Apparently the principal target of 1898's aerial bombard-
ment, this district has recovered swiftly, with looters and
opportunists strangely absent. Inhabitants attribute their
neighbourhood's good fortune to a local philanthropist, a
doctor who protects the area.

8) PROFESSOR MORIARTY'S AIRSHIP

Since plummeting into the Thames near Limehouse Reach
in 1898, the late Professor James Moriarty's airship has
proven intractable, despite frequent salvage attempts. Its
conversion into an 18th century-style 'prison hulk' is currently being considered.

9) FREEMASONS HALL, VAUXHALL

While architecturally an acquired taste, this riverside landmark is an undoubted benefit to the community, as the
worthy fraternity within are believed to occupy themselves
mainly with organising charitable jumble-sales and similar
altruistic activities.

10) INVASION MEMORIAL PARK

At London Bridge's southern end, this small memorial
garden contains a monument to the military dead of 1898's
invasion. A Martian tripod has been rebuilt into a children's
play area, albeit one shunned by children.

THE MURRAY GROUP, CORRESPONDENCE, 1899-1913

Following the successfully-routed Martian invasion of August, 1898, the group for by Wilhelmina Murray earlier that year was almost completely defunct. With Hawley Grif and Henry Jekyll both dead and Captain Nemo having resigned from the unit, Miss Murray apparently felt that there was little point in continuing as team leader to a team whi no longer existed. Being in addition emotionally exhausted after the events of the pre ous few years, she elected to retreat for some time from the world into the pleasant c fines of the matriarchal ladies' commune Coradine in the northwest of Scotland. Mr All Quatermain, the only other member still remaining out of the initial group, stayed in London, living at the team's former headquarters in the British Museum's private wing keeping a low profile since he was at this time still believed to be dead by the gene public.

This state of affairs prevailed until the Summer months of 1899 when Murray, who been in correspondence with her older colleague, was prevailed upon to let him visit h in Coradine, whereat he forwarded to her the proposition that she should return to her employment with the Crown, who had a foreign jaunt in mind for both of them. Perhaps becoming bored with the unending calm of Coradine, Murray accepted and in August she embarked along with Quatermain for the United States, there to investigate unsettling reports concerning the New England town of Arkham, Massachusetts. Returning during the September of that same year after some unpleasant exploits, Murray and her elderly com ion next commenced investigations into the communitarian Phalanstery movement, then bu recently established in the western English county Avondale.

The couple were involved in undercover operations at the Avondale Phalanstery for almost a year, and did not venture overseas again until mid-August, 1900, when the pai set out for Africa on an assignment that required them to find and test the immortalit bestowing waters of a pool or fountain said to be located somewhere in the British Protectorate of Uganda. It proved to be a hoax, possessing no life-giving properties a all, and also proved to be the final quest of Allan Quatermain, the venerable explorer dying in the lost last of Zuvendis during the first months of 1901. Seemingly not faze by her bereavement, Wilhelmina Murray next took up with the explorer's long lost son, a named Allan, whom they'd met in the Zuvendian capital, Milosis. She returned to Englan with her new companion in July of that same year, where the pair became embroiled in v ious domestic issues that would occupy them until February of 1906. 1901 saw a visit t the incarcerated lunatic Dr Eric Bellman at an asylum in Oxford, while between 1902 an 1903, Miss Murray and the junior Quatermain were on Ireland's west coast. 1904 and 190 entailed travels within England, including a visit to the recently-resurfaced brother Mycroft Holmes at his home in Fulworth. At last, in March, 1906, the couple were dis- patched to Russia on a diplomatic mission, strengthening ties in preparation for the Anglo-Russian Convention, forged the same year, that was to govern Tibet, Persia and Afghanistan.

Their travels took in most of Asia, and it was in Tibet that they met an individ of uncertain gender who purported to be the selfsame Orlando who has been referred to the annals of this team throughout its various incarnations since at least the sixteen century. Travelling home to Britain with this person by way of the Arctic territories, they reached these shores during April in 1907, where the trio would remain for quite some time. This was to be the genesis of what has been referred to as the second Murra team. In various adventures over those next years, Quatermain, Murray and the individu who professed to be Orlando gathered other members to their group, including the refor thief Anthony John Raffles and the then-fashionable "psychic sleuth," Thomas Carnacki. was this ensemble who responded to Carnacki's premonition of a catastrophic foreign-in gated raid on London coinciding with the Royal Coronation of His Majesty King George V in 1910. During these escapades the fellowship encountered a dockside hotel worker and sometime prostitute named Diver, of whom we know very little save that she apparently became a regular associate of Murray's second team during the first two or three decad of our current century.

In 1912 this resurrected team was active in the north of England, journeying to France the following year for an encounter with French counterparts "Les Hommes Mysterieux" in natural caverns underneath the Paris Opera in 1913. With Europe on the brink of war, the group's preferred means of communication, namely picture postcards, would become impractical, forcing its members to relay their messages by other means. However, in the fifteen years that until then had passed since the inception of the Murray team, British Intelligence amassed a sizeable collection of such postcards, with representative selection here included on the following pages. We feel that these are c uments of some importance in that they, however sketchily, fill in some of the gaps am the team between the conclusion of their most famed early adventures with the ending o the Mars invasion in late 1898, and their later exploits after the Great War. As such, the ephemera presented overleaf can only aid our fuller understanding of this semi-legendary assembly, and, increasingly, the worrisome phenomenon they have become.

My Dearest Allan,

Of course you may visit me in Coraline, you silly thing. The ladies reserve their contempt for local men, so you're quite safe. I hope you have news of fresh work, as I fear I'm getting rather fed up of women. Do write soon.

Yours affectionately, Mina

To

Mr A. Q.
C/o Private Wing
British Museum
Bloomsbury
London W1

(postmark: SCOTLAND 7:45 PM JULY 1899)

Dear Bond,

We've crossed most of Africa looking for Ayesha's city, and have found directions to it here in Fantippo. I think we could get there in a fortnight, with weather permitting. Must admit, am greatly enjoying my return to Africa. Have never felt better.

Yours,
Quatermain

C. Bond
c/o Freemason's Hall
Vauxhall Cross
London SE11
Great Britain

(postmark: FANTIPPO 3:30 PM DEC 27 1900 AFRICA)

Bond—

Coming home immediately. Met one R. Carter who took us to a ruin near Dunwich - beastly business. Mina almost abducted by some-thing ghastly, and now very feverish. If you or Holmes had any idea this might happen, I'll horsewhip you to within an inch of your lives.

Quatermain

MESSAGE

LORIMER E. BRACKETT
ARKHAM, MASS.

ADDRESS

Campion Bond
c/o Freemason's Hall
Vauxhall Cross,
London SE11
Great Britain

(postmark: BOSTON, MA SEPT 8 5 PM 1899)

POST CARD.

Dear Mr Bond,

I have dreadful news. Uganda's "pool of life" didn't work, and poor Mr Quatermain has died here in Zwendu, although I've met a young, long-lost son of his, which is some consolation. Please excuse the jerky handwriting as I am currently racked with grief.

Yours sincerely, Wilhelmina Murray

Mr Campion Bond
c/o Freemason's Hall
Vauxhall Cross
London SE11
Great Britain

(postmark: ...DIS FEB 3 1901)

My Darling;
Susan is dreadful, but I've met the gentleman I came here to visit. Yes, it's really him. He showed me his bees, and I'm sure I gave the impression of being an awe-struck schoolgirl hanging on every word. Will be home soon.
With all my love,
Mina

To
Mr M. Q. Jr.
c/o Private Wing
British Museum
Bloomsbury
London W1

Postmark: FULWORTH 11 AM MAY 12 1904 SUSSEX

Dear Mr Bond,
I'm uncertain if you will actually receive this, but our posts tell me their postal service is very good. We're all three in good health and are currently guests of Toylanda Queen. Will explain when we arrive home in perhaps a week.
Yours most sincerely,
Wilhelmina Murray

Mr Campion Bond
c/o Freemason's Hall
Vauxhall Cross
London SE11
Great Britain

Postmark: TOYLAND TOWN POST MARCH 10th 1907 — KISS-1

ОТКРЫТОЕ ПИСЬМО
ИНОГОРОДНОЕ.

Shangri-La Sept. 5th, 1906

Bond-Purchased this card in Octavia, but am posting it from a Tibetan lamasery, where we've just met a fascinating young woman who claims to be Orlando, both Prospero and Gulliver's associate. We expect to be returned to Moscow with her by year's end. Please advise.
Yours,

Quatermain Jr.

Мѣсто для адреса.

C. Bond
Freemason's Hall
Vauxhall Cross
London SE11
Great
Britain

Grands Magasins de la VILLE DE SAINT-DENIS
NOUVEAUTÉS
Faubg St Denis et Rue de Paradis - PARIS

Dear Tom,
Well, it's over, though in truth they very nearly finished us. Fantômas was a horror, and the albino almost as bad. Whether the European war you foretold has been averted or not, we shall see. We'll all be home presently, my dear friend. Yours faithfully,
Orlando

Mr. Thomas Carnacki
c/o Private Wing
British Museum
Bloomsbury
London W1 -
Great Britain

Postmark: PARIS 4:15 11-8 1913 BOSQUET

Zwielicht-
Helden

nce the formation of the first Murray group in 1898, which involved the supposedly dead Captain Nemo, a figure well
to the French, in the retrieval of Dr. Henry Jekyll/Mr. Edward Hyde from a Paris address, it may be supposed that
nch authorities have been in some measure aware of the existence of a team of extraordinary individuals, convened
British Crown for purposes of espionage, sabotage and security. While information received by British Intelligence
ts that the French may have been discussing the formation of a similar ensemble from as early as 1901, there is no
ce showing that this was accomplished until mid-1911, when an increasingly desperate French government decided to
amnesty to several personages who had until then been seen as enemies of mankind. France had initially been scorn-
England's reliance on such mentally aberrant personalities as Griffin, Hyde and Nemo, but it would seem that in the
t to form a unit of their own, they had reluctantly reached the selfsame conclusion, namely that in this area of
ment, fiends are both more plentiful and more effective than are heroes.

is now believed that "The Mysterious Men," as they were known informally, were first convened as a response to
irmed reports of a German conspiracy intended to bring war to Europe. Germany, it later transpired, had assembled
clandestine group of unusual individuals by as early as 1909, and it is indeed possible that this Teutonic group
some part in the sinister activities that plagued the coronation of King George VI in 1910. The German group, based
newly constructed Berlin Metropolis, included deviants as bad as or else worse than any in the French or English
ns. The criminal mastermind Mabuse seems to have done most of the thinking for the team, aided by a mesmerist
Caligari, with other members, if reports are to be believed, including a mesmerised assassin and an unlikely sound-
nale automaton and her creator, one Dr. Rotwang. Learning something of this group's activities, the French at last
d on their policy of amnesty, and set about constructing their own league of monsters and peculiarities.

eir first recruit was also the group's senior member, megalomaniac and innovatory aeronaut Jean Robur, France's
led "Master of the World." Initially inspired by the exploits of Captain Nemo, if reports are to be believed, Robur
d to become a science buccaneer in the element of air rather than that of water, and as a member of the fledgling
team proved invaluable, especially in providing much of the team's weaponry and transportation. It may be that it
obur who suggested the ingenious criminal mastermind Arsene Lupin as a prospective member of the formative
ble, since the aeronaut had on occasion, in his private correspondence, voiced his personal admiration for the so
"gentleman thief." At the time however, Military Intelligence suspected that the French planned an assault upon their
counterparts, and that they had included Lupin as way to cancel out any advantages afforded to the British by the
at British born "gentleman thief" Anthony Raffles was a member of Miss Murray's second group.

e three other members that comprised the French team were more problematical, in that at least Lupin and Robur
d to cleave to some strict moral code, however idiosyncratic and outlandish their behaviour may have appeared to
eir three teammates, on the other hand, cannot be said to have shown the first vestige of morality in any of their
, and in fact do not appear to be entirely human in the normal definition of that term. The international arch-villain
eur Zenith, for example, was a pure albino who used drugs that overcame the weaknesses of his condition and indeed
d him physical abilities beyond the ordinary. Even this chalk-white near-superhuman, though, seems like the very
of humanity when we compare him to his teammate, the unnerving Nyctalope. This creature, more some new,
ticated breed of animal than man, had beating in his breast a manmade heart superior to the human model. He
breathe with equal ease in both our normal atmosphere and also underwater, and his eyes were such that the most
n, impenetrable darkness seemed to him as brightly lit as if in the full glare of noon. The Nyctalope's monstrosity was
ed, for the most part, to his physical abilities and his appearance, for in terms of sheer inner monstrosity one strug-
imagine any mind or heart more genuinely alien than those belonging to the final member of this Gallic team, the
r Fantomas.

ven at this extremely early juncture of his long career, the archfiend Fantomas already had the blood of scores of
nts upon his hands, about which fact he scarcely seemed aware, much less concerned. It also seems he was preco-
in the guarding of his true identity, in that those few early acquaintants of Fantomas who lived to tell the tale could
etween them give an accurate description of the man. Robur describes the archfiend as "a masked man of unusual
rtions in that he was not high-built but rather seemed broad-set and dense, fostering an impression of tremendous
" whilst Wilhelmina Murray gave her own impression of a figure that was "quite preposterously tall and thin, at least

some seven feet in height. Other than that I have a memory of some kind of black mask, I have no other recollection face at all, which seemed to me a dark, miasmal blur." Her colleague A. J. Raffles even ventured the suggestion that, least in his perception, something in the voice and movements of this quite demonic being seemed to indicate that Fantomas might be a woman. All, however, were agreed that the most noticeable aspect of the archfiend's presence the sense of unrelenting dread that he engendered. Even the usually composed Miss Murray stated that she'd "never as scared as when it had me cornered underneath the Paris Opera. Fantomas, I think, had me more frightened than been of my Romanian Count, who, it seemed to me, at least had once been human and known human passions. Fanto in contrast, was a thing; had always been a thing." Whatever the true nature of this most dangerous individual, his pre ence in the ranks of the French team was undeniably just cause for alarm.

Not until almost a decade later did British Intelligence manage to piece together what had in all likelihood been true order of events concerning the encounter between these "Mysterious Men" and Murray's team. It seems events w first precipitated by the Germans, Doctors Caligari and Mabuse, who were then working on behalf of Germany, at leas ostensibly, whilst secretly pursuing personal agendas whereby each might profit from the war they hoped to bring to Europe. When they learned that the French had at least some faint inkling what was going on and were preparing the team of misfits as a counter measure, Caligari and Mabuse decided to retaliate with subterfuge. Using a potent mixtu Dr. Mabuse's wiles and Caligari's mesmerism, they contrived to lead astray the English and the French intelligence com nities alike with the dissemination of false information, so that each believed the other's team of extraordinary agents plotting against their opposite numbers on the channel's far side. In this way, embroiling both the French and English teams in conflict, Germany was free to further its ambitions without fear of foreign interference...or at least to furthe ambitions of Doctors Mabuse, Rotwang and Caligari with their shadowy associates, the noxious group referred to by t Kaiser as "mein Zwielicht-Helden."

Complicating matters further for the second Murray unit, during 1912 the "ghost hunter" Carnacki had encounters some form of spirit that allowed him brief, fragmentary visions of the future. These included glimpses of his colleague battling their French counterparts in Paris and terrifying vistas of a Europe caught up in the horrors of the First Worl Whilst both these portents would prove accurate, with hindsight we can see that our mistake was to assume that the visions were connected in some direct, causal way. If the young Quatermain or Murray had been present they might have been so quick to leap to these conclusions, but as it transpired the pair were off globe-trotting on their own du that year, having first visited the tomb of Launcelot up in Northumberland and then set out for Europe, passing throu nosferatu-haunted peaks of the Carpathians to holiday upon the coast of the Black Sea, near to the kingdom of Evarc Thus it was that only the supposed "Orlando" and his friends Anthony Raffles and Thomas Carnacki were in residence ensemble's British Museum hideaway when first the threads of this apparent intrigue came to light. The premonitions ed to Carnacki were soon supplemented by the artful propaganda of the Kaiser's "Twilight Heroes," leading our intellig appraisers to suppose that France was planning to provoke a world war through the agency of their crude copy of th Murray team. Consequently, Wilhelmina Murray and the junior Quatermain were called back from their idyll in the clos months of 1912, and by the February of the following year the whole team, save for Carnacki who was by then feveris embarked for France intent upon confronting their French imitators.

The disastrous opening skirmish in this confrontation took place on the 23rd of February, 1913, when the four-str Murray group attempted a balloon-assault upon the airship of Jean Robur, possibly with the intent of recreating the s tactics they'd successfully employed in 1898 to board and incapacitate the airship of the late Professor Moriarty. Jean Robur, however, was no first-time aeronaut as the Professor had been, nor was his craft powered by Cavorite, which had dismissed as "unscientific." In addition, Murray's second team consisted of four relatively ordinary human individu lacking the weaponry of Captain Nemo, the ferocious strength of Edward Hyde or the unique abilities of Hawley Griffin that time convinced by the misinformation campaign waged by Germany, believing England to be the aggressor in this action, Robur simply shot them down before they came within a half-mile of his craft. Crash-landed in the wilds of ru France, having against all odds escaped their swift, flaming descent with only minor injuries, the quartet opted to atte their next approach by stealth and to this end next made their way to Paris. There, in rented rooms not far from the Morgue where they had first encountered Edward Hyde some fifteen years before, they planned their next moves while the same time investigating the Parisian underworld, with A. J. Raffles trying to track down and thus outwit his rival master-thief, Arsene Lupin.

The Murray team were not aware that Lupin had been set as bait by his superiors in crime, the demon Fantomas deadly, pallid Monsieur Zenith. In this manner were the team lured to the Paris Opera on the night of March 14th, 1913 when the establishment was crowded by its patrons. Finding no trace of the French team, Quatermain and Murray arg over where best to commence their search, the argument apparently concluding with Miss Murray storming off in fros silence to pursue some female intuition of her own and leaving her three male companions to debate amongst themse the merits of a search inside the Opera house against those of a sortie to the building's rooftops. Finally, Orlando and young Quatermain elected to explore the upper reaches of the Opera's exterior while A. J. Raffles with his burglar's ex tise slipped into the crowd-packed interior to see if he could spot Arsene Lupin amidst the throng. Failing to do so, h checked out the building thoroughly and, with a knack for finding secret doors and panels, soon discovered hidden sta that led down from the Opera's basement area, seemingly into the earth.

Meanwhile, Wilhelmina Murray had decided to investigate a rumour that she'd lately come across in her extensive ings, this pertaining to vast natural caves existing underneath the Opera building, where some thirty or so befor monstrously disfigured madman Erik had resided while he carried out his terror campaign as the Opera's so-called "Phantom." Having read of this intriguing subterranean space just two years earlier in a book written about the crime. Miss Murray found her way down into it through a surrounding tunnel system underlying most of Paris. Here she was fronted by the frightful quartet of Lupin, Robur, the Nyctalope and Fantomas, along with the belated realisation that sh walked into a carefully-sprung trap.

the same time, above the Opera house, Orlando had been set upon by Monsieur Zenith, there on the precarious
ıs where a pounding rain had just commenced to fall. Despite the fact that his claims to have fought at Troy and
ry Plain are clearly bogus, the ambiguously-sexed Orlando is undoubtedly a fighter of considerable experience, yet
himself hard-pressed by the albino's onslaught. When his pale and gloating foe spoke of a bomb concealed beneath
era house, Orlando was just able to relay this news to Quatermain, watching the combat helplessly from balconies
unable to assist Orlando in the struggle against Zenith. Quatermain burst instead into the Opera's main hall and
nced the presence of a bomb beneath the building, trying to find A. J. Raffles in the subsequent stampede and panic,
thout success.

neath the opera house, Miss Murray had been hunted down by the inhuman Nyctalope, who was untroubled by the
ess in which Murray stumbled blindly. Rising from the underground stream that the frightened woman splashed
h in the hope of baffling her pursuer's more-than-human sense of smell, the Nyctalope dragged Murray underneath
rface where he breathed with ease while she, quite understandably, had greater difficulty. When Miss Murray managed
ak free he followed her back to the surface to resume his murder attempt, at which juncture A. J. Raffles, who had
n fortunately happened on the scene, shot the amphibious abomination in the chest. (Since it would seem the
ıpe survived this shooting, we can but surmise that Raffles' bullet failed to penetrate the creature's artificial heart,
unded form perhaps retrieved by Robur and Lupin, who similarly seem to have survived the Opera's subsequent near
ation.)

ying to escape from the dark, subterranean caverns, Raffles and Miss Murray had a hair-raising encounter with the
ng Fantomas, which was ended when the villain uttered, in unaccented plain English, the two chilling words "I win,"
; he detonated the explosives hidden elsewhere in the Phantom's former lair. Up above, despite the younger
rmain's attempts to clear the building, some two hundred people were killed or else injured in the blast, which saw
de of the afflicted building subside into empty space beneath the Opera house. Up on the roof, the battle between
and Orlando was concluded indecisively by the collapsing building, with Orlando barely managing to leap to safety as
ınework underneath his feet gave way. Both he and Quatermain helped dig bodies from the Opera's rubble, but
: to find either Raffles or Miss Murray amongst the survivors, feared the worst. Not until some days later were they
ed with the pair, who had escaped the conflagration through the sub-Parisian tunnel system by which Murray had
ıble to locate the cavern in the first place. Quatermain at first chose not to credit the pair's tale of having been
d for three days within a subterranean Graveyard of Unwritten Books or an underground land lit up by luminous bal-
suspecting that it had instead been some romantic interlude between the couple that was the true cause of their
Feelings in the group being thus strained, to say the least, all were returned to London and their museum headquar-
ıoping that they at least had somehow managed to avert the world war glimpsed in their friend Tom Carnacki's
natural visions. We assume that in their victory the French were likewise hopeful that the plot to wreck the peace of
e was thus over with, allowing Germany's nefarious "Twilight Heroes" to pursue this goal uninterrupted.

the First World War that followed the next year, both Murray's team and their French counterparts were to lose
ers, with Jean Robur's airship shot down at the battle of the Somme and A. J. Raffles giving up his life on the front
. Ypres. "Les Hommes Mysterieux" would seem to have disbanded shortly after the conclusion of the war, with Military
ıence failing to receive fresh information on the unit since that time. There is some evidence that Kaiser Wilhelm's
:ht-Helden" were, in one form or another, operating as late as the early 1930s, but failing confirmation of such
ırs we conclude that Murray's team were the sole group of extraordinary operatives extant upon the Earth by the
of World War II, after which time the Murray group itself broke contact with the British Government and fell into
·rity.

iis summary contains all of the useful information that's available on foreign versions of Miss Murray's league. If,
er, further detail or clarification is required then do not hesitate to get in touch through the regular channels.

Live Big Brother.

ɔmmes
ɘrieux

WHAT HO, GODS of the ABYSS By
The Rt. Hon. Bertram Wooster

F riendship can be a rather sticky wicket now and then, as when one's anxious to assure one's chums that one does not regard them as a hideous embarrassment, when actually one rather does. Old hands amongst you will have no doubt guessed ahead that the source of my discomfort was that same Augustus, he of the Fink-Nottles, whom I've previously lamented in these pages. The occasion was a dinner thrown by my Aunt Dahlia at her Brinkley Court dive, off in Worcestershire, and I was trying to pay attention to the conversation of my Aunt and her unusually Bohemian guests, while at the same time shooting furtive peeks at Gussie, seated at the table's end.

He sat there with spoon poised between his dish and mouth, which hung even more slackly open than was usual, staring at the piece of cutlery as if he didn't have the first idea what he was looking at. Fearing he'd shove it in his eye, I gave a complicated cough in Morse code as a distress signal, which worked after a fashion in that Jeeves glided as if on casters to my side, though it turned out he hadn't cottoned on to my Morse code and feared instead that I was going to choke to death.

"I'm all right," I gasped out *sotto voce* as Jeeves brutally compressed my sternum in a harsh remedial manoeuvre of his own device, "It's Gussie. Look at him, for heaven's sake! He wiped his lips on a bread roll a moment back, and now he's trying to eat his napkin. Go and see if he's all right, Jeeves, there's a good chap, otherwise that beastly business with the copper cylinders will all come out in front of Auntie and your friends from the museum, and then we should have a right to-do."

It strikes me that there maybe some of you out there who do not count yourselves amongst the various ne'er-do-wells and publicans who've hung upon my lips for previous yarns and thus won't have the faintest what I'm on about. Perhaps I should go back and start from the beginning, as they used to make me do if I should be caught cheating on cross-country runs at dear old Malvern House, when I was younger. I suppose this current business all kicked off when I received an invitation from my Aunt to spend the summer helping her with some odd jobs at Brinkley Court. I should point out that we are not discussing my regrettable Aunt Agatha who uses battery-acid as a gargle and shaves with a lathe, but rather my Aunt Dahlia, an altogether more agreeable and lively proposition, who insisted that she did not mind at all if I should bring along my erstwhile pal, the aforesaid Gussie Fink-Nottle, to assist me and provide companionship whilst I was at my arduous labours.

"Yes, by all means bring Drink-Bottle with you. The estate's a jungle at the moment, and if both of you young oafs get eaten by wild swine while clearing it, I'm certain that society will be doubly grateful," were her exact words, as I recall them.

Anyway, with Jeeves in tow, Gussie and decamped for Worcestershire and Brinkley Cour where we discovered to our horror that Aun Dahlia had not exaggerated in the slightest whe comparing the estate's grounds to an Amazonia forest. Frankly, if you ask me, she'd been rathe modest. The gazebo and the tennis court were bot entirely lost from view beneath an overgrowth tha pressed against the lofty windows of the drawin room, blocking the light, and making matter worse it looked like there were nasty foreign weed amongst the tangled mass, including one variet with thick and sticky petals that looked just lik tongues, if tongues were eighteen inches long an violet, and another that was lit up brighter than m wristwatch after it got dark.

"Honestly, aged relative," I sputtered at my aun when I confronted her, "you can't expect me an poor Gussie to trim that Sargasso for you. Where' that groundskeeper you hired a year or two ago that Yankee chap from Massachusetts o Pocahontas or wherever he was from? Peabody wasn't it? Or has he joined some new groundskeep ers union and come out on strike? It really is to bad."

Aunt Dahlia gave me one of her affectionat sneers in reply. "Oh, shut your vacuous trap, yo work-shy lout. Poor Mr. Peabody has bee wretchedly ill this last six months. The poor ma can't even come out of his groundskeeper's she since his condition took a sharp turn for the worse He sleeps in there at night between the sacks of fer tiliser, I expect, and don't you dare suggest that I ge rid of him. That man has been a font of knowledg when it comes to folk traditions from rura America, which I believe that I may write a piece o for *Milady's Boudoir*."

This was a weekly periodical, intended for th sensitively reared, of which my Aunt was the pro prietor. I looked her in the eye and said "Tish-tosh, which I am not afraid to state that I intended as cut. I informed her that I had not realised rural fol traditions were now such great shakes, and that next supposed she would keep hens and take up Morris dancing, although I confess I didn't put quite as smartly at the time and when I turne indignantly upon my heel to go and have a wor with this Peabody fellow I collided violently wit Gussie who was standing right behind me, grinnin pointlessly like an unreasonably happy cod, out o politeness. Leaving Gussie there to beam uncom prehendingly through Auntie's well-intentioned mortal insults, I stormed proudly out past a bore looking Jeeves into the grounds, only to find mysel instantly lost amongst the towering, vaguely lep rous foliage. Only by some wonder did I find m way, within approximately half an hour, to th groundskeeper's lodge that was perhaps two hun dred yards away from my Aunt Dahlia's front door

burst in, in high dudgeon, and prepared to give
his idler Peabody a fair piece of my mind, of which
have a good few pieces left to spare, despite what
everyone who knows me cares to say upon the
topic.

"Now look here," I raged, "this simply isn't on.
The place is overrun with all this fancy rot that
you've imported, and the smell in here would choke
a horse. Are you by some chance keeping iguanas
without my Aunt's knowledge?"

It was awfully dark within the spacious hut (a
symptom of Peabody's illness, as I later learned,
had made him sensitive to light), but I could just
make out the poor fellow out as he sat motion-
less in what appeared to be a cast-off and dilapidated armchair on the room's far side, shrouded by
gloom. The moment that he spoke it was quite evident that his complaint had also left him with the
most intolerable sore throat, so that I was reminded by his rasping buzz of a badly-concluded boyhood episode in which I had attempted to collect
fifteen live wasps inside a cocoa tin.

"I apologise for the unpleasant odour," he began,
"but it is caused by my condition, which I think
today maybe a little better. As for the unusual
weeds you mention, be assured that our great bene-
factors from beyond the abyss find it a most com-
fortable habitat, and that its blossoms shall with
certainty attract the Shambler in Darkness."

I supposed he meant Aunt Dahlia, who sometimes keeps odd hours and has a tricky hip, and I
must say that hearing him explain things in a plain,
straightforward manner like that made the whole
thing seem entirely reasonable. In fact, the fellow
had such a persuasive, deucedly engaging way
about him that I pulled a sack of fertiliser up to
perch on and sat down to listen to him chin-wag
for an hour or more. He was a marvellous old character, with all the colourful and slightly baffling
turns of phrase you tend to get from an American.
He told me about friends of his who came from
Yuggoth, which I would imagine is some town in
Massachusetts, or perhaps an outpost like Rhode
Island since he specified it was "beyond the rim."
He made it sound a jolly interesting place, at any
rate, and even offered me a trip there with, as he
said, my intelligence contained in an appropriate
vessel. I imagine *The Queen Mary* was the vessel
that he had in mind, and I'll admit to being flat-
tered by the way he'd noticed my intelligence on
such a short acquaintance, since it is a quality that
far too many people seem to overlook.

He rattled on like this for absolutely ages, telling
me about all these retired chaps that he knew, "old
ones" as he referred to them, who'd apparently
been overseas or somewhere, but were anxious to
return here "when the stars were right." I believe he
mentioned an endearing rogue called something
like "Cool Lulu," which to my ears sounded like it
might be a Red Indian name, who seemed to lead a
leisurely, agreeable old life, sleeping and dreaming
at a place called Riley, possibly a reservation of
some kind. Peabody also mentioned some old goat
who had misspent his youth so badly that he had a
thousand young, which to me sounded like impressive going in anybody's book. There were odd
morsels of homespun philosophy amidst all this,
much of it far too brainy for the likes of me, especially the bits about the three-lobed burning eye
and how the screaming tentacles of retribution
would surely sweep the human pestilence from off
the Earth, but by and large he made what I expect
was quite a lot of sense.

When finally I had to tear myself away, the dear

old thing asked me my name so that he could
arrange my trip to Yuggoth, Massachusetts, safe in
"an appropriate vessel." Here he nodded to some
dusty copper cylinders on a high shelf that I'd
assumed contained weed killing preparations or
the like. I didn't have the foggiest idea what he was
on about, so nodded knowingly in lieu of a reply. I
must confess that I was starting to regret having
seemed so enthusiastic when he'd made the invitation earlier of a trip to the United States, and I'm
ashamed to say that when he asked my name I said
it was Fink-Nottle, but that he should call me
Gussie.

It was almost midnight when Jeeves managed to
locate me by my faint, despairing cries, hopelessly
lost amidst the partly phosphorescent vegetation. I
recounted to him much of what the groundskeeper
had told me and his usually unruffled brow creased
with a frown of concern, notably when I was going
on about the Indian chief or whatever he was, this
Great Cool Lulu who spends all his time asleep at
Riley. Jeeves appeared to recognise the name from
somewhere, and suggested he might get in contact
with a remote cousin of his, on the Silversmith side
of his family, who worked as deputy curator for the
British Museum, which, Jeeves fancied, had
employees of some kind who were ideally suited to
investigate extraordinary matters such as those he
seemed to think were currently unfolding at my
Aunt's estate. I told him that as usual he was making far too much of things that in all likelihood
would turn out to be wholly innocent, and then
retired to bed, knowing that Gussie and myself
should be up early the next morning, to begin the
Herculean labours that Aunt Dahlia had made the
chief condition of our stay.

I tossed and turned all night, racked with a
strong yet inexplicable conviction that my room's
geometry was somehow faulty, even though if I'm
entirely honest I'm not sure exactly which one's
algebra and which one's geometry. If I'm wrong
and geometry's the one with all the letters, then I
mean that my room's algebra was wrong.
Whichever one it was I hardly slept a wink and so
was less than chirpy when at first light my Aunt
Dahlia instructed Gussie and myself to clear an
area that was equivalent in its dimensions to the
misplaced tennis court. Asked why, she told us that
she had invited friends to visit for an outdoor
soirée, folklore enthusiasts like herself, who would
be driving down that evening from homes in nearby Wales or from the town of Goatswood, close to
Brichester, for the occasion. Why my aunt required
so large a patch of weed-free ground on which to
hold her barn-dance or whatever she intended I
had no idea, but as a general rule of practice I've
found with my aunts it's usually better not to ask.

By noon, when we paused briefly for some
roast beef sandwiches and barley-water, Gussie and
I had done a first-rate job, if I say so myself, with
half the space we were to mow and to make tidy
done already. Hacking through an undergrowth of
vivid yellow creeper that to all appearances was
quietly suppurating, Gussie gave us both a scare
when he discovered a dead animal, considerably
dead mind you, amongst the jaundiced shrubbery.
It was, we estimated, three or four feet long and
roughly barrel shaped, its head resembling an elab-
orately ugly starfish and some ghastly tattered
things that jutted from what we assumed to be its
torso, these resembling fins or wings but fearfully
decomposed, so that the whole monstrosity ponged
to high heaven and our eyes were watering as we
discussed what it might be. I guessed, perhaps a lit-

tle feebly, at a cow that had been through a combine harvester, while Gussie thought it might be some deceptively flesh-like rare sprout or cabbage like Vegetable Lamb of Tartary, though neither of our explanations seemed entirely likely and at last we simply buried it and got on with our hoeing.

As we neared our work's conclusion at the first approach of dusk we found ourselves not far from the groundskeeper's lodge, from which there intermittently came bursts of the metallic insect buzzing that I'd heard the previous night, which I assumed must be poor Mr. Peabody clearing his throat. Gussie inquired as to the nature of my conversation with the sick New Englander the previous night, seeming quite captivated when I mentioned the groundskeeper's offer of a holiday in Yuggoth, Massachusetts, and particularly when I told him of the frozen methane mining that I'd been assured was the community's main industry, which to Bunny's way of thinking made it all sound rather swaggering and adventurous, a little like the Klondike. We resumed our work, finishing before dark when Auntie's guests arrived, and a peculiar lot they were. I was so fagged out from the struggles of the day and my entirely sleepless night before that I elected to retire directly to my room, though Gussie thought he might stay up a while and have a poke around to see if he could find Aunt Dahlia's liquor cabinet. I wished him luck and went to bed, where scarcely had my head made contact with the pillow than I fell into a deep and dreamless snooze.

It must have been soon after midnight when I was awakened by the simultaneous agencies of vile subhuman chanting from the garden and a grim-faced Jeeves shaking me doggedly by the lapels of my pyjamas. While I made a vain attempt to chisel open gummed-up and reluctant eyes, Jeeves told me that the experts from the British Museum had arrived and were downstairs now trying to decide what they should do about my aunt, who, it appeared, had taken a severe turn for the worse. I was halfway through asking my manservant what he was suggesting with his last remark when the repulsive moaning from outside began again, this time with my Aunt Dahlia's voice distinctly audible above the guttural slur of her associates. To my bewilderment her wild entreaties seemed to be directed at the Great Cool Lulu, Mr. Peabody's elderly Indian friend, who I had until then assumed was still in Riley and enjoying his lie-in. Jeeves handed me my dressing gown and ushered me downstairs, still half asleep, where in the drawing room were gathered the quartet of individuals that my startlingly well-connected servant's cousin had alerted to the fishy goings-on at Brinkley Court.

They were a dashing crew, I must say, even if they did appear to have a girl in charge of them, a pretty little thing called Min, with steely eyes and a thick muffler around her neck despite it being then the stifling height of summer. With her was a wiry gentleman around her age, whom she called Allan, and another person, called Orlando Something, who despite his deep voice and deportment looked to me the very spit of Gussie's fatuous fiancée, the appalling Madeline Bassett of the limpid eyes and weeping-spasms. Rounding out the foursome was an older man who introduced himself as Tom Carnacki, and who seemed to be regarded by the others as rather an expert on the sort of business going on within my aunt's estate, whatever that might be. He asked me a barrage of questions, most of them concerning my quite innocent and genial chat with Mr. Peabody on the preceding evening.

When he'd finished, he and his companions gave each other shifty looks of great significance before the filly in the scarf fixed me with her somewhat disdainful gaze and started to address me.

"Mr. Wooster, we believe your aunt and her companions to be in thrall to a force not unlike mesmerism, a force directed, it is likely, by whatever kind of entity is posing currently as Mr. Peabody. Far from teaching them about the rustic folklore of America, I fear he has inducted them into an occult brotherhood, and that these dismal wailings from outside are rather loathsome incantations to the cult's foul deities. We would, with your permission, interrupt their ceremony before its intended purpose is achieved. We shall, of course, endeavour to prevent harm from occurring to your aunt or to her visitors. May we have your assent in this?"

I nodded eagerly although I hadn't understood one word in four of what she'd said. She had such an old-fashioned air about her for a mere slip of a thing and such a stuffy turn of phrase that I was terrified she might explain it all again if I failed to agree. This seemed to do the trick, and she with her three male companions marched outside to see what on earth my Aunt Dahlia was playing at, after admonishing both Jeeves and I to stay within the house since she could not give guarantee as to our sanity or safety if we ventured out of doors. No sooner had we heard the front door slam behind them than I wondered, with a sort of miserable presentiment of doom, why Gussie hadn't been alerted by the uproar and come trotting downstairs to enquire what all the fuss was over. Alarm mounting in my voice I turned, as I so often seem to do on these occasions, to the maddeningly competent and level headed Jeeves.

"I say, Jeeves, I've just had a nasty notion pop into my noodle. You don't for a minute think that even someone as devoid of gorm as Gussie would go blundering out alone into a hoodoo ceremony, do you? Tell me that you looked in on his room and that he's drunk himself into insensibility, Jeeves, there's a sport."

Jeeves seemed to close his eyes in weariness or possibly refusal to accept the likely circumstances that we were entangled in. After some moments, when he opened them and spoke he almost sounded thoroughly fed up with me and Gussie both, though I expect it was the tiredness that gave this impression. "Sir, I am reluctant to point out what we both know to be the truth, which is that young Fink-Nottle has all the survival instincts of an accident-prone lemming. I indeed made bold enough to look into his room, but he was nowhere to be seen. I fear he will be almost certainly involved in whatever manner of unpleasantness is going on outside, and furthermore I fear it is incumbent on us to assist him."

This was just the sort of thing I'd feared that Jeeves might say, but I reluctantly agreed to follow him outside into the mayhem and cacophony, in which we passed unnoticed. As we came upon the clearing where my Auntie and her guests were holding what she'd called an outdoor soiree, Jeeves gasped out an oath that I have never heard him or, now that I think about it, anyone else use before. He warned me that I should not look, but all his warnings came too late as I beheld a vision more nightmarish yet than any that I'd hoped to see in this world or beyond.

My aunt and all her pals were twitching and convulsing on the clipped grass, foaming at their mouths and jabbering in tongues, with not a stitch of clothing on between the lot of them. I'd feared

at Morris dancing might result from all this folk
adition lark, but naturism really was the limit. So
ansfixed was I by all the unexpected, vigorously
rashing flesh that I did not immediately register
e shrieking and inhuman form that reared above
e scene with bloodworm tendrils writhing at the
ntre of its starfish face, from which the torn and
per like visage of Mr. Peabody still dangled, flap-
ng mournfully. The foursome from the Museum
ere in combat with the brute, the girlish-looking
ap Orlando hacking gamely at it with a large and
rribly impressive sword while simultaneously Mr.

arnacki bellowed out what might have been
me form of ritual banishing. The other two,
ost sensibly in my opinion, simply shot at it
ith matched revolvers. While I gawped at all
is, Jeeves had noticed that poor Gussie did not
em to be amongst the writhing nudists, and sug-
ested we might find him in the groundskeeper's
ow evidently empty hut.

As usual, Jeeves was bang on target. There in
e pitch black sat Gussie with an object resting
n the table next to him which I at first assumed
be half of a coconut then realised with a
artled yelp was actually the top of Gussie's
ead. My manservant drew in his breath,
en sighed and spoke.

"I feared as much, sir. If what I have heard
f these abominable creatures is correct, Mr.
ink-Nottle's most essential self is at this moment
eing carried to the place called Yuggoth that they
entioned, possibly some other planet or dimen-
on, in the confines of a copper cylinder. Put sim-
ly, sir, I fear they have removed his brain and left
im here like a boiled egg that's had its top sliced
ff."

"Oh bother, have they really? Do you know, I
hought that I was feeling muzzy."

Gussie sat up slowly in the armchair, lifting one
and gingerly to feel around inside his open and
emonstrably deserted cranium. His goldfish eyes
azed up imploringly towards my manservant. "I
ay, you couldn't fix my lid back so that it wouldn't

show, Jeeves, could you? If Miss Bassett saw me like
this I should never hear an end to it."

Wearing a look of incredulity that bordered on
the insolent, and muttering about a tube of glue he
thought that he might have, Jeeves led the pair of us
back to the house past what survived of Auntie's
soiree. The remains of what I cannot help but think
of still as Mr. Peabody were being wound in oilcloth
and transported to a rear compartment of the
motor car in which the foursome had arrived by
the man Allan and the indeterminate Orlando,
whilst Carnacki and the woman wrapped my dazed
Aunt Dahlia and her accomplices in blankets as
they led them gently back indoors. It was quite evident that Auntie didn't have the first clue what had
happened, yet possessed enough innate good
breeding to invite her rescuers to dinner on the
evening following, which brings me back to where
I started this unfortunate account, with Gussie
spooning pea soup into his breast pocket while I
hoped no-one would notice.

As it happened, no-one did, not even Miss M.
Bassett after she and Gussie were eventually reunit-
ed. As Jeeves pointed out when we'd successfully
concluded that nerve-wracking meal, the young
Fink-Nottle had devoured his napkin on at least
five previous occasions, and at least this time had
spared the napkin ring.

"Gosh, Jeeves. Do you suppose that this new
Gussie might be an improvement?"

"Sir, I find it difficult to picture how it could
conceivably be otherwise."

Down at the table's end, Gus rapped upon his
forehead with one knuckle, opening and closing his
delighted-looking mouth to modulate the ringing,
hollow sound it made. I beamed at Jeeves and he
allowed himself a faint smile in reply.

It was all going to be tickety-boo, in the most
meaningful interpretation of that phrase.

"Eldritch old business this, eh,
Jeeves?" I asked him, eruditely.

"Quite so, sir," he murmured
in response. "Quite so."

...acki bellowed out what might have been
...e form of ritual banishing. The other two,
...t sensibly in my opinion, simply shot at it
...s matched revolvers. While I gawped at it
...s, Jeeves had noticed that poor Gussie did not
...em to be amongst the writhing nudists, and sug-
...ested we might find him in the groundskeeper's
...now evidently empty hut.

As usual, Jeeves was bang on target. There in
the pitch black sat Gussie with an object resting
on the table next to him which I at first assumed
to be half of a coconut then realised with a
startled yelp was actually the top of Gussie's
head. My manservant drew in his breath,
then sighed and spoke.

"I feared as much, sir. If what I have heard
of these abominable creatures is correct, Mr.
Fink-Nottle's most essential self is at this moment
being carried to the place called Yuggoth that they
mentioned, possibly some other planet or dimension, in the confines of a copper cylinder. Put simply, sir, I fear they have removed his brain and left
him here like a boiled egg that's had its top sliced
off." ...oh bother, have they really? Do you know,
...as feeling muzzy,"... in the armchair, lifting o...
...side his open a...
...fish

ello? I WONDER, COULD I SPEAK TO MOTHER, PLEASE?

IT'S WILLIAM.

YES, HELLO? I-IT'S BILLY.

WELL, IT'S JUST I'VE HAD SOME VISITORS. THEY THOUGHT YOU MIGHT BE AFTER THEM.

YES, THAT'S THEM. SAID THEY WERE HEADED FOR THE SPACE PLACE UP IN BIRMINGHAM.

YES, TOMORROW SOMETIME.

I-I'LL GET MY POSTAL ORDER AS USUAL?

Yes. YES, THANK YOU.

THANK YOU, MOTHER.

Cheerio.

RIGHT, THERE WE GO.

NEXT STOP, BIRMINGHAM.

WELL, NOT QUITE. WE'VE GOT TO CHANGE AT VICTORIA, NOT THAT THAT'S ANY GREAT HARDSHIP.

SUPPOSE NOT.

DID YOU REMEMBER TO PACK THE DOSSIER?

THAT? OH, I LEFT IT AT THE BED AND BREAK-FAST.

CLOT. WHAT DO YOU *THINK?*

KEEP LEFT

Sorry.

DO YOU KNOW, I'D FORGOTTEN THAT BR COURT BUSINESS U LAST NIGHT.

SO HAD I. AND WHAT ABOUT THAT F NOTTLE CHARACTE

WELL, THAT'S A *JOKE.* IT HAS TO BE.

NOBODY COULD WALK 'ROUND WITHOUT A BRAIN.

REALLY? MOST OF WOOSTER'S SET SEEMED TO MANAGE IT.

YES, THAT'S TRUE.

HOW SHALL WE REACH DUNBAYNE FROM BIRMING-HAM, INCIDENTALLY?

TRAIN, I EXPECT.

WE'LL CROSS THAT BRIDGE WHEN WE COME TO IT.

BIRMINGHAM
SPACEPORT

WOMAN'S DREAM

NORMA DESMOND

BIRMINGHAM
SPACE PORT

SPACE LINE

Ooh,
THIS LOOKS
MODERN. IS
THIS IT?

NO, THIS
IS JUST THE
ENTRANCE
FOR CARS AND
COACHES.

WE'LL BE
THERE IN A
MINUTE.

Ta
very much,
Guv.

YOU'RE
WELCOME.

GOD, IT FEELS
GOOD STRETCHING
MY LEGS, THAT TOOK
HOURS.

SO,
WHICH WAY IS
IT, THEN?

WELL, I
EXPECT WE JUST
FOLLOW THIS
LOT.

DON'T GET
YOUR HOPES UP,
EH? IT'S PROBABLY
NOT AS GRAND AS
WE IMAGINE.

MM. YOU'RE
RIGHT. I MEAN
CAVOR'S ROCKET
WAS TITCHY,
WASN'T IT?

WELL, YES.
AND THE SPACE
PROGRAM'S ONLY
JUST RESTARTED
AFTER BIG
BROTHER.

I MEAN,
WHEN YOU THINK
ABOUT IT, IT'S BOUND
TO STILL BE IN
THE EARLY...

Bloody
hell.

MY GOD, MINA. LOOK AT IT.

I REALLY NEVER THOUGHT I'D LIVE TO SEE THIS.

IT'S... IT'S QUITE SOMETHING, ISN'T IT?

I'LL BET EVEN CAVOR NEVER DREAMED THAT THIS WOULD HAPPEN.

I DON'T KNOW. I SUPPOSE AFTER THE MARTIANS IT WAS INEVITABLE THERE'D BE A BIG RUSH TO GET INTO OUTER SPACE, BUT EVEN SO...

ARE THERE *GUIDES* HERE, DO YOU THINK? THAT CHAP LOOKS OFFICIAL.

UM...EXCUSE US? I'M AFRAID WE COULD USE A BIT OF HELP WITH ALL THIS. ARE YOU A SPACEMAN?

NOT ME, MISS. ORDINARY AIRPLANE PILOT GARY HALIDAY AT YOUR SERVICE.

WHAT WERE YOU LOOKING FOR?

NOTING IN PARTICULAR. WE WERE JUST INTERESTED IN ALL THESE *ROCKETS.*

WELL, I'M ONLY A ROCKET-SPOTTER, REALLY, BUT I KNOW A BIT.

TAKE THAT ONE OVER THERE. THAT'S THE PANCAKE EXTRA-LARGE SERIES FOUR.

L 4

"Pancake"?

YES, WELL, THEY NAME *NEW* MODELS AFTER HOW THE PREVIOUS ONE ENDED *UP.*

THERE WAS THE MUSHROOM CLOUD X-L THE SHRAPNEL X-L 3...IT A *TRADITION.*

HAN ON

...ARE THES THE ONES W ROBOT *PILO*

OH YES. WE READ ABOUT THAT WHEN WE WERE IN THE *STATES.*

SEE-THROUGH ROBOTS MADE OUT OF PERSPEX OR SOMETHING, ALL WITH NAMES LIKE RONALD, OR RODERICK...

THAT'S RIGHT. THE X-LS ARE AMERICAN MADE.

WELL, I SUPPOSE THEY'D *HAVE* TO BE. WHO *ELSE* THINKS "EXTRA" STARTS WITH AN *X?*

THANKS EVER SO, MR. HALIDAY. YOU'VE BEEN JOLLY HELPFUL.

ANY TIME MISS. YOU ENJOY THE OF YOU VISIT.

HE SEEMED A NICE BLOKE.

WHAT ELSE DID YOU WANT TO LOOK AT?

OH, I DON'T KNOW. I WAS HOPING WE'D SPOT SOMEBODY FAMOUS, LIKE MORGAN OR HAWKE OR SOMEONE.

YOU KNOW HOW I AM.

WELL, YES. YOU'RE A SQUEALING BOBBYSOXER OVER ANY SQUARE-JAWED CHAP YOU'VE READ ABOUT IN A MAGAZINE.

DON'T COMPLAIN. I'D NEVER HAVE BOTHERED WITH *YOU,* OTHERWISE.

LET'S GO AND LOO IN THE GIFT SHOP.

Do e have to?

LOOK, I THOUGHT I MIGHT GO AND FIND OUT WHERE WE CAN GET A CAB TO BIRMINGHAM STATION.

FINE BY ME. I'LL SEE YOU BACK HERE IN TEN MINUTES, SAY?

KEMLO

INTERPLAN POLICE PATROL

10/-

COULD I HAVE THIS, PLEASE?

OH, THE WESTMINSTER ABBEY FUNGUS-ASTRONAUT KEYRINGS? YES, THEY'RE VERY POPULAR.

THAT'LL BE ONE AND SIX, LOVEY.

Oops, sorry.

NOT LOOK-ING WHERE I WAS GOING.

QUITE ALL RIGHT.

THIS IS IT? THERE'S NO OTHER WAY OUT?

NO, OTHER THAN STRAIG UP TO RUDD VENUS.

COME ON LET'S HAVE BUTCHERS, SHALL WE?

STONE THE CROWS! WHAT A SPREAD, EH? STILL, I THOUGHT THERE'D BE MORE GREEN IMMIGRANT BASTARDS.

WE'D BETTER SPLIT UP. I'LL TAKE THIS SIDE.

Hmm.

BIT OF A CASE, YOUR GODFATHER, ISN'T HE?

OH, HE'S VERY SWEET REALLY, IF YOU DON'T GET HIM STARTED ON THE JEWS.

HE PROBABLY
...S GOLDSTEIN
...E FOUR-MINUTE
...E AND ALL
...THAT.

HE'S VERY PROTECTIVE OF YOU, Y'KNOW. WARNED ME OFF, AT ANY RATE. SAID HE'D MURDER ME.

He did what?

YESTERDAY AFTERNOON, HE TOLD ME NOT TO TOUCH YOU.

I'D JUST MADE AN INNOCENT REMARK ABOUT YOU BEING A BIT OF ALL RIGHT...

Oh, HAD you?

WELL, EVEN SO, HE'D NO RIGHT TO SAY THAT.

...HIS WAY OF
...NG OUT FOR ME,
...CT. HE PROBABLY
...S I'M RATHER
...ERABLE TO OLDER
...AT PRESENT.

DID YOU KNOW MY FATHER DIED EARLIER THIS YEAR?

Uh...no, I didn't. I'm sorry.

IT WAS A BIT SUDDEN. HEART ATTACK, RIGHT AFTER HIS BIRTH-DAY LUNCHEON IN MAY.

THAT'S TERRIBLE.

I WAS OUT OF THE COUNTRY DURING MAY, IN JAMAICA SORTING OUT SOME MAD DOCTOR FOR THE COUSINS.

...I HEARD ABOUT
...YOU'RE QUITE
...US AMONGST
...SECRETARIES,
...U KNOW.

OR IS THAT INFAMOUS?

HA. YOU SHOULDN'T BELIEVE EVERYTHING YOU HEAR.

SHOULDN'T I?

Oh dear.

AND HERE'S ME DESPERATELY HOPING IT WAS ALL TRUE.

CHRIST ALMIGHTY. WHAT HAPPENED TO THIS POOR LITTLE BUGGER?

Welcome ho-ome.

Welcome ho-ome.

TALKED WITH A LISP. OTHERS BIT IT TO DEATH.

Welcome ho-ome.

Welcome ho-ome.

GIFT

Oops. Sorry.

NOT LOOKING WHERE I WAS GOING.

'TE ALL 'GHT.

WAIT A MINUTE.

YOU'RE MURRAY.

MURRAY OR HER DAUGHTER.

HH...

S-SO YOU KNOW INDIAN WRESTLING, DO YOU?

WELL, YOU JUST WAIT UNTIL I...

dy

Oh, bloody Hell...

MINA?

MINA, HOLD ON!

Hnuh?

OI! NOT FAST, JACK FLASH!

WHAT?

WHAT THE BLOODY HELL DO YOU THINK YOU'RE...

LANGUAGE.

THERE'S BLESSED LITTLE KIDDIES ABOUT.

THEY DON'T WANT TO HEAR YOUR EFFING AND BLINDING, DO THEY?

Unnh...

B-BUGGER YOU...

DIDN'T YOU HEAR W I JUST SA ABOUT T KIDDIES

ARE YO AFTER ANO THICK EAR, ARE YOU

...DEAF...

AAAGH!

OH SUFFERING JESUS...

URRRLH...

MINA, HANG ON! I'M COMING!

LEAVE HER ALONE, YOU BULLYING COW!

I'LL KNOCK YOU TO NEXT TUESDAY!

ALLAN, DON'T! SHE KNOWS JUDO O SOMETHING...

Right.

HERE WE GO.

SECRET SERVICE. GET OUT OF THE CAR.

GET OUT THE FUCK CAR!

FUCKIN ADA. ALL MATE, A RIGHT

What...?

SOMEONE'S SHOOTING. IT'S...

OH, BUGGER. THAT LITTLE PRIC VAUXHALL. TELL WHAT, LEAVE TO ME.

WHAT? WHAT DO YOU MEAN?

AAAAA!!

DEAD SLOW
SPEED LIMIT
8 M.P.H.

BLOODY
~~OD SHOT. HAVE
~~U KILLED HIM,
~~O YOU THINK?

NO SUCH LUCK. HE'S STILL MOVING.

WE'VE GOT TO GET OUT OF HERE, LOVE, AND SHARPISH.

YES, WELL, I THINK I'VE GOT THAT SORTED OUT.

THIS WAY, ONTO THE EXTRA-LARGE SERIES FOUR.

THE FRUITCAKE? DARLING, NEITHER OF US CAN FLY A BLOODY THING LIKE THAT...

~~UALLY, IT'S
PANCAKE,
~~E DON'T
~~E TO FLY
IT.

THESE ARE THE ONES WITH THE VOICE-CONTROLLED ROBOT PILOTS, REMEM-BER?

QUICKLY, GET ON BOARD SO I CAN SHUT THE HATCH.

MINA, ARE YOU SURE THIS IS GOING TO WORK? I DON'T REMEMBER HALIDAY SAYING THE ROBOTS WERE VOICE-CONTROLLED.

HE DIDN'T. I READ IT IN THAT DIRTY MAGAZINE YOU BOUGHT IN AMERICA.

STAGMAN, WASN'T IT?

~~GMAN'S NOT
~~TY. THEY PUBLISH
~~ES BY KENNASTON,
~~T, CHAPS LIKE
~~ THAT...

...WHICH YOU DIDN'T *READ* ANY MORE THAN YOU READ THE *ARTICLE.*

YOU JUST OGLED THAT "MONTANA WILDHACK" FLOOZY IN THE FOLD-OUT BIT.

LOOK, I KNOW YOU WEREN'T MUCH ON THE STAGMAN CLUB, ALL THOSE GIRLS WITH THE DEER ANTLERS, BUT...

ALLAN, HUSH A MINUTE.

UM... HELLO IN THERE?

HELLO?

WEL-COME-A-BOARD.

I-AM-RO-GER-THE-RO-BOT.

WHAT-IS-YOUR-COM-MAND?

...unkhh...

JIMMY? JIMMY, ARE YOU ALL RIGHT?

OPEN THAT BLOODY HATCH. WE'RE SECRET SERVICE. OPEN IT AND LET US ON.

URRH...

W-WE CAN'T, GUV'NO LOCK FROM INS THESE THING DO.

OH, FOR CRYING OUT LOUD!

WE'LL HAVE TO SMOKE 'EM OUT, THEN. IT'S NOT AS IF THEY CAN TAKE OFF ANYWHERE.

YES THEY CAN, GOV. THESE ARE AMERICAN JOBS, THESE.

ALL MOD CONS AN' THAT.

MINA...

GHUHUHHH...

DAMN.

LOOK, WE CAN COMMANDEER A HELICOPTER ONCE WE HAVE RADAR FIND OUT WHERE THEY'RE GOING.

COME ON, BEFORE THEY'RE OUT OF SIGHT.

Here's Wharton's pet project, as mentioned at the funeral. More fate than morph eh? And then poor bun-scoffing Bessie's trouble keeping her mouth shut. Anywa congrats on the top job. You've worked hard for it.

My very best,

Bob

WHEN THEY SOUND THE LAST ALL CLEAR
The Murray Team 1939-1945

During the twenty year hiatus between the first and second World Wars, the second Murray team, reduced in numbers, would seem to have kept a considerably lower profile. After the death of A.J. Ra in the trenches of WWI the group consisted of a core membership comprising Miss Murray herself, the junior Allan Quatermain, the "eternal ambiguity" professing to be Orlando and the increasingly haunte seeming Thomas Carnacki. This was the ensemble responsible for the intervention at the bedevilled Bri Court estate in Worcestershire during 1930 and various similar exploits throughout the remainder of t decade.

Despite the apparently limited membership, Military Intelligence is currently of the opinion tha during this period the Murray group may have been covertly associating with other unusual individuals while keeping these associations a secret from their Vauxhall employers. In light of Murray and her leagues' deliberate disappearance immediately following WWII, it may be that throughout the several y preceding the war, Murray was stealthily building an extended network of contacts, unknown to the int gence services, as preparation for her planned desertion. While our knowledge of these further clande liaisons is by definition limited, we are reasonably sure that they included meetings with a former u side prostitute named Diver and, at one point, a self-styled "surrealist sportsman" who suffered fro chronic dwarfism and whose first or last name was apparently Engelbrecht. They were also seen with wh witnesses referred to as "a stocky, unkempt Negro with a very deep voice," and are believed to have occasion utilised the services of a Mr. Norton, an intelligence gatherer sometimes referred to as "t prisoner of London." According to discarded notes in Murray's handwriting found at the team's former British Museum headquarters, Norton is confined, in a third dimensional sense, within the limits of t city and its suburbs, whilst in the dimension of time he is able to explore the metropolis without restriction, from its past to its uncertain future. Indeed, perhaps supporting this outlandish claim, have discovered documents from as far back as the late Glorianian period that make mention of a stra attired "Master Nortonne," this individual's description matching closely with descriptions of Miss Murray's sometime colleague.

Whatever the true extent of Murray's circle of acquaintances during this time, there remain few facts concerning her adventures that we can regard with any certainty. As an example, Murray filed re for the Spring months of 1937 claiming that she and her two associates, Orlando and the younger Quatermain (Carnacki having by this time retired from active service for health reasons), had spent t period investigating subterranean territories beneath the North of England, while according to surveil sources they were travelling by submarine towards the Arctic circle when they vanished, only reappear roughly three months later to hand in a clearly fabricated false report of their activities. Departme analysts who specialise in Murray and her doings have suggested that her team may have been looking f the fabled group of islands north of Orkney that have been referred to as "The Blazing World." Naval Intelligence has searched in vain for this location several times, commencing in the 18th century, an time and time again it has been proven that the islands are no more than tall tales spun by windswep inebriated Orkney fishermen, or possibly hallucinations caused by sudden venting of undersea gasses i area. Despite the utter lack of any evidence which might suggest that they exist, these islands seem have become almost a pathological obsession for at least three incarnations of the special team. Poss "The Blazing World" has entered into the group's mythic history, almost an article of faith, with the unauthorised trip to the Arctic seen in this light as some debased form of religious pilgrimage, but the very least the incident and its subsequent cover-up should serve to illustrate the furtiveness an

BE LIKE DAD -
KEEP MUM!

unreliability of Murray and her team during these years. At the outbreak of war in 1939 the Murray team by consisted of just three impressively vivacious, youthful seeming members, which is to Miss Murray's credit as she according to our records in her early sixties at the tim The charlatan who posed as the historical Orlando seemed more eager for the coming conflict than his teammates, claiming to have "not been in a decent war for centuries and as a consequence enlisting in the RAF, where he prov at least to be a skilled and creditable fighter-pilot wi genuine thirst for battle. Murray and the junior Quaterm meanwhile, were occupied in carrying out a number of important missions, both abroad with missions that entai espionage and sabotage, or on the home front dealing wit the spies and racketeering opportunists who were thrivin under cover of the Blitz, such as the apparent dynasty o black-clad burrowing bandits intent upon stealing the Cr Jewels, or an early manifestation of elusive internation criminal mastermind The Voice.

In 1941, Murray and Quatermain were briefly back in London after they'd successfully accomplished the regret but necessary dynamiting of the Channel Causeway when it become clear that Herr Hynkel's forces planned to use th bridge for a full scale invasion of the British Isles. A half-mile section of the bridge, construction of which h only been completed by the April of 1908, was blown to b by the two agents, who were roundly criticised for havin detonated their explosive charges while the bridge was e

WATCH OUT—
DENOID'S ABOUT!

Don't let the Führer get up England's nose!

rather than when it was choked with German troops and tank divisions, as they'd been instructed. Found amongst the notes retrieved from the British Museum's locked wing after those premises had been vacated by Miss Murray and her group were jottings that pertained to Murray's state of mind on her return to London:

"London's taking a hell of a kicking. Orlando, who's back in the city on leave from the air force, says that he's seen worse, and we should have seen Carthage and Pompeii and so on and so on. He got on my nerves a bit, though he's a dear, of course, and it was lovely to see him. It's just, if I'm honest, he's ever so much more agreeable when he's a her. When he's male you can't go very long without being reminded, quite often unpleasantly in my experience, of just how good he is at killing people, either with that wonderful sword (which simply <u>can't</u> be what he says it is) or with any other weapon that man has invented during our young friend's considerable span upon this Earth. He can shoot as well as Allan, which is saying something, and of course he's mastered aeroplanes, which Allan goes green at the thought of. I love Orlando, both of us do in our different ways, and it goes without saying that he's also, over the years of his life, become an extremely accomplished lover. So has she, most definitely. 'F---ing and Fighting, the only two things that I learned which have stuck with me,' as he so memorably put it. But then you think about him hewing men down in their dozens, in their thousands down the years, at Troy, at Salisbury Plain, in every bloody field men ever read of in their history books and shuddered, and you realise that he's a bit of a monster. Possibly that's how you get when you've watched the utopias and the wars without end come and go. Perhaps that's how we'll all end up, given another century or so. As shuffling troglodytes who can't even be bothered

n sentences, or as raving barmy as Ayesha. God, I'm in a cheerful mood tonight.
It's probably just seeing London that's got me all maudlin. Everywhere's a mess, the places that I
o know all blown to rubble for the most part. I walked through the East End today, around the
ect Nicholas Dyer's creepy church at Limehouse in the streets where our Chinese foe had his lair,
n what seems another world entirely. How we dressed then, how we thought, all of it blown away just
o much confetti when the wedding's done. Whole streets had been reduced to rubble by the bombing,
l over the buildings that were still standing there were posters telling everyone to 'dig for vic-
or 'be like Dad and keep mum.' These precious, stupid little English jokes and catchphrases when
e been pulling the bits of their neighbours and their relatives out from beneath the bricks and
g beams only the night before. God, I'd give my life for these people, and that's saying quite a
my case.
As disturbing, in a different way, was the discussion that I had with the Prime Minister when I was
to Downing Street, with Allan, somewhat earlier this evening. I'm afraid to say that the Prime
er had obviously been drinking, and what we had imagined was intended as a highly confidential ses-
f debriefing after our explosive escapades out on the channel causeway seemed to somehow wander into
rming rant. He saw plots and secret societies everywhere, and was especially concerned that there
rogue factions within MI5 who were currently grooming a successor to replace him as Prime Minister
a favourable conclusion to the war. He believed that in all probability the challenge would come
omeone installed by Military Intelligence within the Labour Party, probably someone from a solid
ry background and intensely charismatic with a splendid chance of winning a post war election. Once
ice, the P.M. believed, this MI5 puppet would see in a nightmare dictatorship with every citizen
surveillance, patrolled by Gestapo-like secret police, their every civil liberty suspended.
He broke off with a haunted look there in his bloodshot gundog eyes, as if he'd said too much, and
e of those caber-sized cigars that have the same effect on me as mustard gas. After he'd puffed in
silence for a while he seemed to gather some of his composure. Brushing aside his sinister conspir-
l fantasies as if the conversation had never occurred, he moved on to tell Allan and I the true
for this visit. We were to be despatched to the United States to see what influence we could exert
merica to help us, if not by agreeing to enter the war in alliance with ourselves and Russia, then
st by forbidding the repulsive and lucrative trade between American businesses and Herr Hynkel's
y. It seems a bit of tall order, but I should not mind seeing America again, if only this time we
t compelled to go near bloody Arkham. London at the moment's a depressing ruin, and it might do us
bit of good to get out of the country for a while...and to stay there, if there should turn out to
hred of truth in the Prime Minister's distressing vision of the post war Britain as a beastly
ist forced-labour camp erected on a national scale. Who knows? This might be just the break that
been waiting for."
It is of course a pity that these notes, with their suggestion of a planned desertion, did not sur-
efore Quatermain and Murray had both broken contact with their supervisors and had disappeared into
st American interior. We have had intimations since of their continuing U.S. activities, including
ters resembling the pair occurring in a modern "beatnik" novel, but to all intents and purposes we
ssume that they've defected and will thus not be returning to these shores. Our best hope might be
ggested plan to form a stand-in team, but barring this and until such time as any further informa-
s available as to the whereabouts of Murray and her friends, then I suggest that we consider this
losed.

THE WARRALSON TEAM, 1946-1947

When by 1946 it was apparent that Miss Murray and her colleagues had deserted our employ by going missing in America, MI5 elected to replace the group with surrogates in an attempt to recreate the impact of the 1898 ensemble, widely held to be the most dynamic incarnation of the team. To this end they enlisted the distinguished Women's Air Force Captain, Miss Joan Warralson as team leader, evidently seeking a replacement for the capable Miss Murray. Lacking Captain Nemo and his Nautilus, the engineer and icthyologist Professor James Grey was recruited in his stead, while standing in for Allan Quatermain was William Samson Junior, the son of an Intelligence employee, who'd already proved his mettle in Afghanistan. One Dr Peter Bradey, who'd duplicated the experiments of Hawley Griffin, became a second (and distinctly second rate) Invisible Man, and rounding out the team in lieu of Mr Hyde was a somewhat dilapidated 1930s prototype robotic man of military origin and known as the Iron Warrior. Fraught with tensions from the outset (Miss Warralson's previously unsuspected tribadism and Mr Samson's attempts to recreate the Murray/Quatermain relationship with her being just one example), the new group was disbanded after just one unsuccessful sortie against a pairing of pirate-slaver James Soames and Italian master-criminal Count Zero.

**f Captain Joan
Warralson**

Warralson was used by the War Office as a female role model
. girl recruits during WW1. Not entirely 'as other women,' she
.ed since then with her companion 'Frecks,' apparently an old
hum.

**Mr William
Samson Junior**

After many notable exploits in Afghanistan alongside his deadly
cricket-bat wielding colleague Chung, the younger Mr Samson
resigned from the substitute team when his advances towards
Captain Warralson were predictably rebuffed, and returned to Kabul.

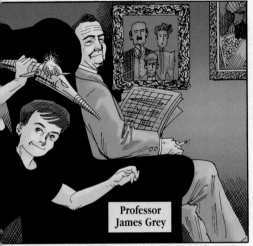

**Professor
James Grey**

r of an impressive swordfish-styled submarine, Professor Grey
l to have been inspired while travelling, during boyhood, upon
inal Nautilus, which apparently rescued him from the attack
illed his parents during the 1898 Martian Invasion.

**Peter
radey**

**The Iron
Warrior**

ting Hawley Griffin's original experiment from discovered
ooks, Dr Bradey successfully achieved invisibility, but was less
sive as an operative due to his compulsive chain-smoking and
ng fits, which, upon numerous occasions, gave him away.

A faintly desperate attempt to lend the new team Edward Hyde's
ferocious power, this 1930s military automaton with its oversized
chopper was dangerous even when switched off. The abortive
Soames/Zero battle concluded with the Iron Warrior's accidental
explosion.

25¢

F-953

She wanted it...
for all time!

THE CRAZY
WIDE
FOREVER

SAL
PARADYSE

Complete and
Unabridged

urped out of a beanery one more warm molecule jigged in a loud gas of sailors an whalers an
 ole fellers an cellarboys all a big comforting Buddha fart sneaked out and leaked to the street
g down Vanness Avenue pungent and not yet diffused in confetti stars exploding weddingcake
nd dimestore night angels who wipe down their counters in sad little ovals glass track bird-
ack through the morgue dust & so forth & so forth into the blue wonder of evening with side-
nrabbled unspooled like a typewriter ribbon got dropped bunchin up inta hillup an trough an
l an the coast of it tempting the feet to a hot trot gavotte where the shoe come down chik on
pewalk chachik chik there's metalpress letters vowel horseshoes nailed onto the soles stamp-
cident prose on the asphalt with every step every bum-stumble footslap tataptap you roll up
r each brow with a peek from the peak at the road rumpled onward to Fisherman's Wharf an
y an the burn o' burlesque bulbs an bars in a glimmery mirrer o' brine what a night what a
what a sigh what a kick in the eye that's Satori to you son an on down you run from illuminate
rom the height from the light the true view and descend into Maya again to the valley an
ed if you don't fergit all what you knew on the brink in the sleep of the deeps badoobeep
 beep where the hunchback horizons crowd in black as crow soot as creosote crouchin like
als then crawled up over the crest creeps that powder blue Dodge with its lamps bright white
ite fine in the damp in the wheezin ole dogfog an rolls in to graze up the curb right ahead and
dead with a shudder right down to the chrome an it's almost some sweet heartbroke waitress
 in sum mattress-jazz moth-sweat motel room when gray railroad dawn tried to peep through
nd from outside with one hand in its baggy tramp pants an the Dodge kills its beams an a back
ncracks like a ladybug's jacket with one corner flakin its paint on the scrape o' the street where
 dinosaur ants struggle hopeless in tar pit trap spilt soda scum an unfoldin out frum sum rear
 a fresh hatched flamingo of movie star nylon she come with a double bass swivel an sway a
jumble of heels on the street there in front of you blockin the way in her second skin skirt feet
in a capital A and her body commences the alphabet of a whole language right there buddy
there not three feet away in this cornerbound crease of the phosphorous Universe with all its
leaders cracker crumbs moonlight an cheese an volcanoes an switchblades an sweepstakes an
en sleeping through trolleycar stops an made new evry immanent immigrant instant the fresh
 of Now Tathagata Now everything Now an yr eyes flutter up zigzag swoop over hipswell an
 an strut an jut bugs to a flashlight her face candlewhite Sunday ice cream its flame curlin out
 wind fudge sauce auburn an likewise the scarf in a twist at her throat tussled also an there in
ttle green glass of her eyes I first see the Forever wide crazy and bottomless em'rald Pacific
onches an corals in columns of weed color light an th' centuries shoalin all solemn like turtle
stical hieroglyph shells through the full fathom five of her stare's Saratoga you fall in an don't
 breath till you drag yrself drippin back out agin back on dry land an she calls you the name
our own Sainted mother bestowed calls you Sal calls you Paradyse tells you she's Minnie but
 mooched ner kicked a gong an the Dodge runs its engine an seen through the wipe o' the wind-
n her man sittin quiet at the wheel with his eyes same as hers full o' years what he shouldn't of
d so they say to get inna the car but yr still in the heavenly swill of the alkahole where alla this
enture in newspulp cologne Captain Easy boots Lone Ranger mask and why not and why not
 yrself careless out on the dice diamond bosom of chance with the rattling stop signs holes shot
 carcass of dark bleeding fire an if in this world we can't trust midnight caprice then what can we
nswer me that you get in an it pulls away into the mystery into yr luck an yr puff an yr life -

) little did we know but Dr. Sachs was settin fer us even then an comin through the night air
 of cotton candy snatch an motor oil in paranoiac radio transmissions relayed back n forth on
 oach aerial conducted by electrolytic sweat o' bad Ed Dunkel rollin lushes at the depot an the
  traitor spoff o' married cops collectin payments offa wrung out gals what work the docks - Ole
 achs slips wi' the ease o' breeze roun' Chinatown in alley steam firecracker strings o' light an
 n flags or lazy drums his mand'rin hypodermic fingernails on mustard mess an mottled mica
 restless fidget of a diner 4AM with outside pale light in the east an all the few first birds the
 osos warbling silver frills to flounce an bounce off an ionosphere all hunkered down aginst the
 afore o' sunrise heavy with the heavy lonely radio ham voices o' retired storekeepers school-

teachers stump preachers drunk in Delaware in Denver wireless whales what wail their woes a
the deep salt ether squeal an pop an static crackle flak an Dr. Sachs stirs alla that into his sch
an snaps it back lips smack the whole great sparklin dark burns like a warehouse in his throat
way down damn if he don't know everthin ole Dr. Sachs gets it fum taxi hacks clairvoyant stri
pinkface laundry girls in hot cross ponytails gattlin' Chinese fum out the backroom ole queen
prin over cocktails stuff what blind bums mumble in their sleep an evryone's his snitch his s
nothin gets by Dr. Sachs not even words spelt out from alphabet block accident by harmless ba
dribblin in their bibs their cribs he reads it all reads the whole town five minits top t' bottor
some big stone Mayan sports page stubs his gage an goes an flows he's opium tar it skitters
foil he's printers ink what pools and pours in gutter subway ditch n drain he slides acro
rooftops sizzles in the wires an aerials an dawgs awl whine n teaheads git the fear n Dr. Sachs
black above the chimney stacks sad sacks the railroad tracks what run like suicide into the wee
feeds on needs an greeds bleeds into telegraph transmissions scrambles messages to random vc
poetry he is the scrawld phone number what makes lovers fight and I will tell you this of infar
is Mahatma in the Mission district's tinders he makes winos dream that there's no cigarette
between their fingers uz they slobber down to sleep he leaps fum little children's wardrobes he
blues the news the bruise round momma's eye the East Saint Louis Toodle-oo comin fum s
where in a shut down barber shop with dead hair like n autumn onna checkered floor he is the
of Shame his voice a gila monster lisp all stept-on leaves an creak o hangin tree an muttrin
through potters field an some say as his tailored suit's got pictures painted on all over like a
hoardin men with gator faces Fiji mermaid in a pickle jar a map of Egypt an the martyrdom o b
Cath'rin there on one lapel Jack Dempsey on the other Borgia popes all roun his hatband Lus
sinkin on his fine silk tie his breath is smoke n aniseed an on his white Italian shoes is spats
descent rattlesnake n cuff-links made fum smoldrin meteorites n chews a toothpick nail fum th
cross an Dr. Sachs swells up n swallers all th' fire escape n washin linen silhouetted tenement n
some attic lamp through threadbare curtains n he fills the quilted moonless sky tobacco stair
blottin out the Milky Way an poses like some Sat'day fiend fum RKO fee fie foe fum drui
acrost almighty heaven an by gum there's nothin an nobody he can't reach what with them sj
crabs them peril-yeller claws in evry mortal heart n through the clouds right now right nov
squintin down fer us an our blue Dodge an smiles n shows his marble teeth with names an dat
chiselled on an sure enough his phlegm is green ball lightnin when he spits -

3 Back in the wild ride crankin winder down to flip a butt a tiny red hot acrobat somersaults
towards the smearin streakin road below an gone an sinkin back in an ass-plastrin' bake o Sur
leatherette I'm prop'ly innerduced t' Minnie n her boyfriend English Al who's drivin face all
lit green n Halloween knows all about me me n Dean flat broke n sacred drivin down betwee
big black sheets o sputnik spangled space above Highway beneath us with that white line st
'long its hem unpicked an ravelled out t' destiny n Minnie sez how everythin's a vital miss
they're in *The Thin Man* English Al an she they're Willum Powell n Myrna Loy spinnin abc
globe in diner cars n great cruise liner Queens n limousines avertin villainies n rightin ruin an y
it all the whole thousand n one Arabian nights t' hear her delicate best Sunday china voice wi
its tinkling silverware an what a tale boys what a tale she tells above the motor's satisfied tin
cat purr of lo an ho an long ago in London Town a-drown in deep deerstalker fog an how a mac
fesser an a wily oriental demon come ta blows with airboats spoffin flame down on sum
Victoriolan slum beedum beedeebeedeebeedum n both t' grief they cum n sum say as their sc
feudin yit in grandsons far across the cold Atlantic settled in Amerikee where has the devilisl
nee an offspring sprung son of a son o that inhuman Fu man Dr. Sachs by name a roamer cor
choo choo train down Frisco way they say a fishhook finger sunk in evry pie in evry goose
thigh in evry last gasp sigh n blackened spoon n goon n meat rack smudge muff magazoon the r
pizen e'er distilled swilled through the town's drain veins n straind brains Dr. Sachs by nan
here's the rub bub his ole grandad's foe no reglar Joe but the Napoleon o crime n craft this mac
fesser Moriarty his own grandson his own line all unbeknown aint no one else but Dean machi
mean Dean Moriarty unsuspectin spielin wheelin dealin words in quickfire spit through pill d

onkey wrench flip an be Jaysus hip the very soul o Hip itself wuz in the direst danger dum dum
an that's how English Al an Minnie put it down for me an axed did Dean been seen or where
ere he be an in th' thrall o this appall recall a date not too late right tonight a time a place a rant
me at the Spaghetti Fact'ry in among the nod n bleu French fume cats mumblin masterpieces
ir scrappy armpit beards n Dean hd flipped his wrench an said that he'd be there you under-
maybe git sum student o litrachure back inna sack n Al he looks to Min n spin the Dodge aroun
own bound an ax the way to this event then take off so the burnd up rubber smell like some
on plantation all ablaze all bats n lemurs bustin from its foliage n spark n so into th' vasty danks
k we skwheel an thru th' movin glass n gen'ral worn-out quality o streetlite San Francisco looks
over fum a painted pulp with colors lurid faded deep sincere rose petal maiden aunt pinks a
robber blue all run together in th' rear view n we go t' rip th' Torquemada corset offa treason -

Now he is the very devil Dr. Sachs an wurse he is the champ o' hell ousts Faust whups Krupp
s Nero zero he's Mephrisco Bayzeebub incarnate Lucifornia Satandreas Asmode o Day
odah gla boo zoo bah zo zee zah dirty Pennecost his name in asslick pussyluppin tongues o fuck
n he don't make no pact not wi' juss any two bit purgatory punkass pup o' pah pah pah pah
emonium not Dr. Sachs he deal with top hat hoo hah Haiti cemeterrians shoot craps wit' jack-
ds in Memphis alleyway clinches hiz biz wit' titan ole boy Greek godpappy baby eaters neat 'z
icks in a fix onna four horse apocalix got that great twat o' Revelations turnin' tricks n sells out
nan an babykind to pinkbrain gumball Martians cum fum outta space n places west o' there
e Great Cthula does the hula hula n ole Yoggy Soggy rools n drools n creeps croon n th' chaoz
ls n Dr. Sachs got contacts contracts compacts dun in blud n jiz in cat tears n Death Valley rain
out in smoke fum opium n rum n nun-cum n th' sweet sweet sweat o Dizzy's brow in puke in
n piss on parchmint n papyrus King Tut catgut Cat'lic priestskin on the dried fried hide o Rin
'in does Dr. Sachs n calls his markers in cuz boy tonight's th' night th' snakebite prizefite Mardi
o' mayhem murk n moanin' Macbeth merder comma monstruss masterplans an crapped out
red cornered careless inna cunt hair crosshairs o' this crimminent catastrophe none other than
an machine-oil Dean who broke hearts fixed exhausts charm wealthy widders fum the trees
akin' off his shirt n talk rings round th' mighty dawn at Big Sur n at Berkley with Bull Hubbard
in' innercent as babies inna backseat unna dark dilutin' down inta lagoon blue n laburnum ore
Moriarty who right now right on the burnin' hot Zen billspike o' this moment is all busted
ed concussed n trussed up inna cellar subterraneous n secret unner th' Spaghetti Fact'ry one
wet n glistnin' gray like toad tongue in yer stannard yeller flyshit light you understand n Dr.
s strut down n up n forth n back black whacko cackle thretnin' knuckle crack his shadder flung
ll 'z Plastic Man behine him n in one claw hand a big ole nitemare outhouse needle fulla cali-
d serum look like locust syrup glass gleam ting in lightbulb swing n drippin at the tip plip plip
h Dr. Sachs explain accordin t' sum ole Republic serial script in hiz flophouse fire matchbook
per how this is some Aztec virus junk what's stewed n stilled fum foot long cennipedes n boiled
aniac spines n jimson weed iguana glands blood 'v a screamin schizophrenic syphilitic saint n
how juss one jot o this hot junglerot shot up th' mainline whatcha got is right away alla these
zacoatl vampire dybbuk ghouls an ziggurat-hat gore-drunk gods on welfare homin' in like
in thousan-year ole junkie warhead missuls on that exac' jaggid narco frequency what's now
in yer brainstream n yer bloodstem alla them death jaguars n corn-bloodiers n parrotsnakes cum
in downa waveband slap inside yer head they got 'emselves new handles better threads more
d t' our peasant present time n sticky pastel polyester clime with these Great Old Uns known
lately 'z th' Nova Mob pug-ugly spirits real fun guys fum Yuggoth dun up wid a lick o' paint
nothin wrong widdat so Narlyhooly haunter o' th' dark what done fer poor young Bobby Blake
calls hisself as th' Sublim'nal Kid jumps in an out TV commercials so's ya barely see holds
up say fuck granma an drink pepsi an bow down afore th' Red Chinese an shoot yerself right
this next beer n he ain't but the half of it you take ol' Hastur what they call Unnameable now
improved regrooved answers to Mr. Bradley/Mr. Martin two ole waspy fruits in one suit like
ya fergit ta wind th' camera on double explosure ain't it now n these n all their polterghostly
r simmrin in the cringe o' th' syringe juss waitin' fer ter git banged inna old Dean Moriarty's

veins n brains change alla wirin' round change alla grammer on his pill pop non stop yammer
him nothin' 'cept a smallpox jukebox rattlin toxic tunes Frankenstein propaganda ravin' railin'
solollygagger spoutin word disease Cthulhu fhtargle gargle R'Lyeh n bop virus festrin inna ea
all what listen openin' channels so Sublim'nal crim'nals Mr. Bradley/Mr. Martin n Hamburger
alla rest o these primordial yeggs n cosmic dregs n anti matter bums n beggars can seep i
scooped out skull lay eggs ad jingle caviar control bugs slaver ants is what they are got wireta
yer daydreams sex schemes holy blazin visions in their dogditch convict searchlight beams
yoomanity'll soon be pressin levers in its ratbox gittin monkeyshocks 'z soon 'z Dr. Sachs git
with his expository rant whacks that big hypodoomic spike in Dean then shoves him babblin
stage to rage n roar infect the whole Spaghetti Fact'ry crowd wid sick new language finger-sn
approbation even 'z th' Nova Mob come thrashin down like psychic tapeworm hook itself onna
eye pineal gland the neck hairs stand n juss like that they's in they win n infernal eternal sub
tion c'n begin n Dr. Sachs tracks this way n then that his boot heels clackin onna flags he bra
promises alla this awful an stupendous stuff ta Missus Moriarty's bound-up n befuddled bo
sprawled agin the wall afore him in that fact'ry cella fulla ole I-talian migrant worker ghosts
died fum wheat n semolina lung granson o his granpappy's gratest gaslight grudge n Dean lool
n shrugs as best he can wit' alla rope n' dope n' lack o hope but never unnerestimate nobuddy
gut Master Criminul genes n rag ass jeans like Dean's born onna road wit Burma Shave his
sign born in back 'v a junkyard jalopy judderin through Salt Lake City all that preachin n polyg
juss percolatin in down hiz umbilical n never did stop talkin ever since talkin thru creampuff ca
sprayin flakes in Hector's cafeteria thru tetanus tapwater toothpaste suds in Spanish Harlem talk
cow manure n snow in Colorado n now Denver cannot sleep fer its lost heroes Dean juss s
shrugs up ut Dr. Sachs an right away starts in wid all his piston injin perfect prattle prose "Ye
I am of course aware o all these matters you describe an have in fact give them my full consi
tion but it seems t me there's one thing you're fergettin in all this n what it is is Schopenhauer
said how God is th' creator o the Universe you unnerstand but in th' imminent sense rather thu
transitive that's right so in my comprehension o these facts I must conclude how you n me r
syringe n these spaghetti splinners onna floor n the almighty state o California herself yes yes t
right all busted inna being just this second now with all our mem'ries o Grandfeudin' Fathers
duds dodos Mayan gods n such all come inta existence th' same time n I can't help but think
all this unnermines yer supposition o sum family vendetta immemorial when there weren't n
here but nuthin one half second back you unnerstand n all this spinnin world plainly th' vain d
o illusion which puts me in mind o certin episodes what I may not have previously bin forthc
over these concernin incidents an' items from my disaffected youth like this one Puerto Rica
knew how to blow smoke out the corners of his eyes n suck his own dick back there up in Boon
reformatory..." Dean runs on an on that way he had back then like evry conversation wuz juss
less white line road he'd gotta burn up on his way t' th' celestial Monet smudge o th' horizun
Dr. Sachs sags flags collapses back t' sit on flour bags n ole pasta sacks jaw slack his wicked
hung wiltin fum his wizened wizzerd lizzerd fingertips cain't git a wurd in edgewise an muss
like evvabody else fer Dean t' lose hiz steam what he's got more uv 'n a reverse Chinese lau
what takes clothes in clean n sends 'm back near black wi' bullshit so the mental institution mor
slogs on whilst up above out in the clammy satin glove o San Francisco night there's foetus lig
kickin in th' stretched-thin belly o the sky an trouble backed up out th' drains n sewers like a
o poor rejected baby alligaters all grew up n hungry fer revenge like all of us n the blue Dodge
on non stop thru storm an slap an puddle slop like Continental Op on rum run bloody pulp n t
der n the dark split n th' world undone -

5   Now me an Min an English Al wuz pals in swerve n veer careen screen idol style n while
vileness wuz unfolded we wuz wailin up the wide wet way wit' water droplets wobblin up the
juss like ice skaters lost their nerve an teeterin' back towardsa safety o th' rinkscreen's edg
there's no time ta lose Al's ridin a short fuse o bad news got them minutes left ta save th' planet
hunched in abuv th' wheel he's lookin grim Jim an the baldin' rear tyre squeals the way he feels
tense n juss about t' jump the corral fence o common sense n right then Min starts in ter hum

n humdrum number cum fum offa radio sum croony moonyjoony freshman matin' call what y'
fum Summer afore last *Immortal Love* 'r sum such nuisance nunsince bland n canned out 'v
-kin Bandstand Land n right away Al's big knot shoulder muscle slacks relaxes n he settles back
inna driver's chair cranks downa window lets th' wind slick back hiz hair an dam if he ain't
in t' sing along wit' Min both grinnin now like Dr. Sachs ain't gonna doom damn an destruc-
ean Moriarty n the hole world both right after these commercials n when I'm impertinent enuff
ntion all this smoochy stuff Min sez how while back she n Al wuz in New York where Hyman
non fuck sea-heart sailors inna washroom ut th' Port Authority scream "feed me I'm a Jew" at
s n sing holy holy holy Willyum Blake almighty in th' beat up negro dawn n Min an Al back
sit talkin all one night wid wud-be Hoagy Carmichael song ritin' genwine genie-ass up in sum
ld water tenement next thing ya know they're lissnin onna radio show by late nite firelite glow
it's their life story bin stole whole n stuck inside a song immortal love immortal love immor-
p op op op op op pom an when I heard that an I sore the smile what sparked between um then
w anew thut it wuz true what I'd first seen thur in hur eyes th' crazy wide forever n then English
hits the brakes n takes th' blue Dodge halfway uppa curb out front o th' Spaghetti Fact'ry n
spillin out inta the shuv un shout makin the scene eyes out fer Dean who's nowhere t' be seen
we go low shumblin' downa cellar stair an there right there he is in sideshow Major Domo full
go man go n Dr. Sachs juss settin dazed crazed n amazed wit dat soul-poison icepick hypoder-
ricklin fum its pointy prick there clickin tickin fore n aft atween hiz fingertips n wam bam
ht up English Al's Tom Mix Bill Boyd Floyd Patterson dun up in wun he guns hisself acrost
llar's fungal floor n scraps n slaps n smacks Sachs who snaps back on th' attack both 'v um
slin in spaghetti dust while Min steps in cuts Dean loose wit a switchblade hatpin alla time him
n up his furthermores n heretofores n yesyesyes that's right that's right that way he had you
rstand n alla sudden strugglin' unner English Al ole Dr. Sachs cracks n by accident he jacks all
ake froster fulla fearful fluid fantoms smack right inna hiz own groin his bulgin' eggwhite stare
back n Dr. Sachs start slappin mat n foamin fum the thighs n in hiz eyes surprise to realize how
em Mayan monster boys gonna be teemin streamin inna forebrain backbrain wuss thun Night
spout their virus gibb'rish out his mouth n wid a wild old-fangled strangled cry he bust fum
e celler up the stair hell bent intent on pukin out his pois'nous purple parlance on the patrons
poetry affair but Min's prepared an out her bag she grab a neat no-nunsense needle uv hur own
out as Novocain is what it is havin anticipated as these mental maladies o bygone Yucatan get
d fum head t' head in word o' mouth n Min wades in jumps up on Sachs's back n hikes that
right ouch aw jesus thru his chalky cheek an inta gum n off the scrabblin babblin Doc gets
as desp'rit on he run invade stage n get set t' rage all o th' uncaged Nova mugwumps 'v ar
rn age down onna audience all hushed n reverent n hip but soon uz he tries makin wit' da lip
' inflection an infection plain refuse t' cum struck dum jaw numb lung bum n stunglin nung
g gung bung n the Mayan mind mob mill confused inside o him n cain't git out n Dr. Sachs that
bold gon bad juss stand there globberin n slobberin arms thrashin flashin lites n snarlin' rarebit
meltin in n outta place aroun' him Mr. Bradley/Mr. Martin got three eyes two mouths two
s optical illusion flarin up n gone Sublim'nal Kid inna periph'ral flicker holds up button readin
e Ike then disappear fasser un fasser in a spittin sputtin an spectac'lar pinwheel Djinn-spin
rybody down" scream Min an SPOO! ole Dr. Sachs he blew explodes so goo n grue blue glue
rospinal spew flew all about th' view leave nuttin' 'cept fer yeller smoke a ringin prehistoric
n smell kinda like burnin tooth enamel anna whole Spaghetti Fact'ry crowd stand still n stund
echliss sev'ral seconds 'fore the silence lapses inna claps n finger snaps roars uv applause n
what don't agree that Dr. Sachs man that cat is real gone n San Francisco life goes gloriously
ariously on n me n Dean n English Al n Min head out inta th' parkin lot t' kick a stick o tea
n hardly a sound th' rain let up evvawhere wet n fresh n better yet the cushion clouds unpicked
eadbare stuffd wit stars soon evvabody gigglin like kids Min grin with lazy lapid lids lets Dean
slinky serpent smoke between hr lustruss lappin lips n evry flag o fate n blazin houri o th'
state was shimm'rin in a Bodhisattva bedsheet Borealis shook out like a blessin over Golden
over the gone world wit' its Vaudeville villains n Paramount paragons its stockyard sunsets
crate labels hubcaps children n goodnight n goodnight n goodnight -

My dear Gerry,
Here's the most recent summary of verifiable facts (few) and wild rumours (many) that
cern the Murray team, although I realise that at the present moment you have far more
pressing matters on your plate. I hate to say this, but I really think that Wharton's
great political experiment, the Ingsoc years, has rather run its course and had its ch
And while you know I've always had the greatest confidence in you...look how I looked
after your interests when the problem with H.W. came up...I must say that your attempt
raise the party's flagging fortunes by re labelling it "New Ingsoc," although well int
tioned, is most probably a tactic doomed to failure. I know that you had little choic
but to concede to the Conservatives' demands that they be reinstated as official oppos
tion party, especially with those documents concerning government irregularities and i
galities falling into Tory hands like that, and with that step once taken then I under
stand that furthermore agreeing to demands for an election became something of an
inevitability, but I'm afraid to say I really don't see any way that you can win. Whil
obviously in my official capacity as head of Military Intelligence I remain impartial
look forward to working alongside your successor, on a personal level may I say that I
have always thought of you as a dear pal and will regret that I could not have done m
to avert these difficulties.

Incidentally, I've heard the odd disquieting bit of gossip around Miniluv in Vauxhall
some junior party members, possibly those ghastly oiks at Minitru, are trying to convi
you that somehow either myself or my department had a hand in engineering this whole d
mal business, even going so far as to claim that MI5 had been responsible for the rele
of the aforementioned incriminating documents to the Conservatives. Gerry, I'd like to
think you know me well enough to realise that I'm not that sort of chap, the sort who
treat you as a chum while plotting your demise. Wharton, of course, was the exception,
I know that both of us were in agreement in that instance over how it should be handle
So come on, let's not have any more muckraking, accusations or absurd suspicions comin
between us, eh? I'm your most loyal colleague, Gerry. You know that, and I'd advise yo
to be careful about letting people put about wild stories to the contrary. I say this
a friend who has your own interests at heart.

Returning to the subject of this summary, as I suppose we should, there really has bee
very little fresh material of late concerning whatever is left of Murray and her squad
of odd fish. As you know, Murray and the younger Quatermain were sent out to America i
1941 in order to persuade the USA that it should cut industrial ties with the Third Re
and join the war on England's side. Unfortunately, the then Prime Minister had by that
time been made aware of certain elements within British Intelligence, myself presumabl
included, who intended with war's end to engineer election victory for an ex military
"Strongman" candidate of suitable charisma who'd remodel England along lines which we'
suggested. The Prime Minister, regrettably, hinted as much to Murray just before he se
her and her boyfriend to America, and we believe that this accounts for Quatermain and
Murray's failure to return to Britain with the war's conclusion: having had advance wo
of what was intended for the country, we presume that they elected to go absent withou
leave in the United States rather than come home to the rigours of BB's regime, to whi
they clearly felt considerable antipathy. Adding to this the oft expressed resentment
Miss Murray for the machinations of British Intelligence, we believe that Murray and s
few associates as she has left should now be classified as hostile.

You will note that there are photographs attached to this report, purportedly of
Quatermain and Murray in America, taken on various occasions during the last decade, b
we are reluctant to conclude with certainty that the young couple in the pictures are
duo of misplaced adventurers. For one thing, it is difficult to square the age of the
depicted couple with that of our former agents. When Miss Murray brought the younger
Quatermain back home from Africa to England with her following the unexpected death of
Allan senior, his father, in 1901, both she and her young paramour were in their early
twenties. This suggests that both must, if they are indeed alive, be currently in thei
late seventies. Our inference is that at some point over the last forty or so years
Murray and Quatermain have somehow found the time to raise a family in secret and have
substituted both a son and daughter without letting us become aware of this, or else h
by some other means produced a pair of lookalikes as substitutes. I will admit that ne
ther of these explanations are entirely satisfying, but must serve until such time as
ther facts become apparent.

Whomever the individuals that we have identified as Quatermain and Murray may turn out
actuality to be we do, as indicated previously, have various reports of their activiti
in the United States across the last ten years. Scant references within the opening ch
ters of the here appended copy of The Crazy Wide Forever by S. Paradyse suggest that d
ing the last year or two the couple (or a pair strikingly like them) were in San
Francisco mixing with bohemians and criminals, while elsewhere in this same text it's
implied that our rogue agents were the inspiration for a gramophone recording of the c
rent U.S. type, which similarly is included elsewhere in this dossier but fails to off
any clues to Murray and her partner's whereabouts, being a rather fanciful, insipid an
romantic song of little consequence such as Americans are, one supposes, presently in
favour of.

According to our source, the duo seem to have laid low while in the U.S. for the most
part keeping to small towns dotted about the country such as Maybury or Riverdale and
making only infrequent excursions into metropolitan environments like Central City,
Gotham, San Francisco, or New York. Perhaps predictably there are reports of Quatermai
and Murray seeking out examples of the latest transatlantic novelties and fads, arrang
meetings with contemporary recording artists and, on at least one occasion, socialisin
with the lower echelons of that most startling and deplorable of post war U.S. trends,
the "mystery man" or costumed vigilante set. In New York it's alleged that they encoun
tered the supposed goddess of love called Venus and through her met several minor repr
sentatives of this unusual sub group such as Gotham's by then elderly Crimson Avenger,

star Linda Turner's close associate the Black Cat, mental marvel Brain Boy and a
een-year-old orphan said to draw fantastic powers and abilities from an adjoining
 spatial region or dimension ruled by technologically advanced fly people. Make of
what you will, although the current MI5 position on these U.S. "supermen" is that
are, in every likelihood, a showy and elaborate propaganda exercise of the by now
iar American variety, most probably intended to scare off and put the wind up the
se and Soviets, with their reputed supernatural powers supplied by film effect tech-
ns drafted in from Hollywood.

ncident stands out, from the pair's brief unwelcome stay in Maybury, North Carolina,
sketchily recorded in the Maybury press and elsewhere going unreported, this being
ouple's unsought intervention into local politics and issues of a sensitive and
l nature. Seemingly, a Negro man from out of town had been held in the Maybury jail
rals charges, including an accusation of procuring, with his two white skinned female
plices who were apparently twin sisters from the Netherlands. The Negro, possibly
ring from birth deformities, was at the time described as being little more than five
tall but of enormous bulk and weight with a skin colouring recorded as "matt black"
 it apparently was textured in a manner that did not permit even expected normal
ghts and reflections. More intriguingly, his two reportedly extremely highly sexed
e companions each had a full complement of what were said to be "unusually lifelike
ell engineered prosthetic limbs," suggesting they were both multiple amputees of some
iption, possibly fleeing with their black protector from a touring carnival or freak
such as are still evident in many areas of the West, although bewilderingly the
 is also implied to be "an aviator" of some kind. Indeed, it seems that once Murray
uatermain (if that is truly who they were) had freed this fellow and his harem from
sonment by means of a highly destructive jailbreak, the quintet made their escape in
according to one sheriff's deputy's account as "exactly like one of them there hot
alloons, 'ceptin it weren't." Whatever we may make of this, it stands as the most
led record of the couple's doings in America.

only other member of the team still living during wartime in the 1940s was of course
sex change charlatan Orlando, who indeed had thoroughly distinguished his or herself
e conflict with an eventful stint spent in the R.A.F. Orlando seemingly came back to
n several times on leave during the early 'forties, but would appear to have slipped
tly from view sometime in 1944, as expertly and thoroughly as his former companions.
 she has not been seen or otherwise reported since, although there was a frankly
d rumour that for a brief period the self styled legendary adventurer evaded notice
e novel means of having been against his or her will transformed into an animal by
ery.

ink that's pretty much it for the Murray group, and as I mentioned at the outset of
piece, I'm sure you have more pressing matters on your mind at present though before
ose there was a bit of unrelated business that I thought I should bring up concerning
my own and poor old H.W's old school chum Johnny Night. As you're aware, Night
stries are helping us tremendously with the unusual equipment they're providing for
projects at Port Merion and elsewhere, and even Sir John's teen age daughter Ema
s extremely promising as a department agent in the future. You may also know that yet
her former Greyfriars chap, Al Waverly, is currently constructing an intelligence
rtment under the auspices of the United Nations, and that to everyone's surprise Night
stries received the contract for equipping this new outfit. It appears that the
icans are hopping mad about all this, having expected one of their big companies to
the juicy contract. One of their Central Intelligence lot, F. Gordon Leiter, has made
r that he suspects some English public school old boy conspiracy is swindling Uncle
out of his just rewards. Heaven forbid and all that, but I really feel we've made the
ins awfully shirty over this one and should keep an eye out for U.S. retaliation. The
 obvious way, of course, would be to sabotage Night Industries or even get at Night
how. With this in mind we have him under careful watch and also closely monitor
icans arriving in this country, so I can't see any way that they could pull it off
out us knowing. So basically problem solved, I think.

ay. I believe that's everything. My best to you and Julia, and I'm sure however these
tions go you'll be as right as rain in no time. Chin up, eh?

main, of course, yours most sincerely,   Robert Cherry

Hmm.

SO THAT'S THE END OF IT, THEN.

JOLLY INTERESTING, DON'T YOU THINK?

I SUPPOSE. PARADYSE'S STORY WAS A LOAD OF RUBBISH, THOUGH.

OH, ALLAN. GET WITH IT. NO, I WAS MORE INTERESTED IN THIS *LAST* PIECE...

I MEAN, IT LOOKS TO ME AS IF CHERRY HELPED O'BRIEN BUMP OFF BIG BROTHER AND ASSUME PARTY LEADERSHIP.

DO YOU THINK SO?

I'M ALMOST POSITIVE. CHERRY... OR LIME OR WHOEVER HE IS... PROBABLY EVENTUALLY BETRAYED O'BRIEN, TOO, WHEN IT SUITED HIM.

HE'S POISONOUS FRUIT, DARLING.

THEN THERE'S THIS BUSINESS ABOUT *NIGHT* AND HIS DAUGHTER.

THAT'S WHO SHE *IS*, INCIDENTALLY. I FINALLY *PLACED* HER.

WHAT? FINALLY PLACED WHO?

LITTLE DOLLY LONGLEGS WHO LOOSENED MY FILLINGS BACK A THE *SPACEPORT*.

SHE'S THE LATE SIR JOHN NIGHT'S DAUGHTER.

HE'S THE INDUSTRIALI ISN'T HE?

Was.

THIS AMERICAN CHAP, *LEITER.* THAT NAME RINGS A BELL, TOO.

NOT TO WORRY. IT'LL COME BACK TO ME.

WE MUST BE NEARLY THERE...

YES, YOU'D THINK SO, WOULDN'T YOU? LET'S ASK ROGER.

ROGER, WHEN ARE WE DUE TO TOUCH DOWN IN *DUNBAYNE?*

COR-REC-TION:

CAN-NOT-LOC-ATE-DUN-BAYNE-SPACE-PORT.

THERE-FORE-WE-CAN-NOT-TOUCH-DOWN.

CRASH-LAND-ING-SHORT-LY.

ASH LANDING?
HANG ON...

GER,
'T YOU
ANDING
? I
AN...

NEG-A-TIVE.

OR-BIT-AND-
SPACE-PORT-LAND-
ING-ON-LY.

Oh bloody
hell...

CHRIST. HE'S GOING
TO FLY US INTO THAT
MOUNTAIN.

ROGER, WHERE ARE
THE *PARACHUTES?* OR
THE *JETPACKS?* WHAT-
EVER YOU *HAVE*...

PAR-A-CHUTES-IN-
REAR-LOCK-ERS.

IM-PACT-
FOR-TY-
SEC-ONDS.

FORTY
SECONDS?

ALLAN, FOR
GOD'S SAKE JUST
HURRY, WILL
YOU?

A, I CAN'T
I CAN'T
JUMP OUT
ROCKET...

OH, GIVE ME
STRENGTH. ALLAN,
WILL YOU STOP
WHITTLING?

There...

I'M DREADFUL
WITH HEIGHTS,
YOU KNOW
THAT.

I DON'T EVEN
KNOW IF I'VE
DONE THIS UP
RIGHT.

WE'LL SOON
FIND OUT. NOW
COME *ON.*

WAIT A MINUTE,
LET ME GET MY
CASE.

IT'S GOT MY
GUN IN. I CAN'T
LEAVE...

FIF-TEEN-
SEC-ONDS.

AND YOUR
DY *GUNS!*
RE'S NO
IME!

COME ON.
I'VE GOT THE
DOSSIER...

OH GOD.
MINA, PLEASE
DON'T MAKE ME
DO THIS.

Suit
yourself.

Fucking
hell.

OH,
FUCKING
HELL...

OW! BUGGER...

...OD.

...I...

...GHT I'D

...T. ARE

...N ALL

...GHT?

I **THINK** I'VE TWISTED MY ANKLE. I MUST HAVE LANDED **BADLY.**

Poor love.

COME ON. LET'S GET YOU UP, THEN WE'LL FIND THIS **CASTLE.**

WELL, I SHOULD THINK THAT'S IT **THERE,** ISN'T IT?

OW.

HM. DOES RATHER LOOK LIKE IT, EH?

GOD, I'M STILL **SHAKING.** THAT BLEEDING IDIOT ROBOT COULD HAVE **KILLED** US...

A-ALLAN? I CAN **HEAR** SOMETHING...

OH, FOR CRYING OUT LOUD.

IT JUST NEVER BLOODY **STOPS,** DOES IT?

COME ON.

GORDON BENNETT.

WHAT THE DEUCE HAS BEEN GOING ON HERE?

IT'S THE ROCKET, THE *X-L*. THEY'VE CRASHED THE BLOODY THING.

YES, WELL, WE CAN *SEE* THAT, CAN'T WE. WHAT I MEANT IS WHERE *ARE* THEY?

LET'S PUT DOWN BY THE WRECKAGE. THEY COULD BE DEAD.

BLESS YOUR HEART, EM, BUT NO SUCH RUDDY *LUCK*, I'M AFRAID. THOSE LOOK LIKE *PARACHUTES* DOWN THERE.

WHY DON'T YOU SET US DOWN NEAR THEM?

Right you are, Sir.

SHOULD I HANG ON HERE, SIR?

NO. YOU'RE NOT CLEARED FOR WHAT COMES NEXT. YOU HOP IT, AND WE'L RADIO WHEN WE WANT PICKING UP.

UNCLE HUGO, *LOOK!* I CAN *SEE* THEM! *THERE* THEY ARE!

Oh God. Oh God, they're going to get us...

WE'RE ALMOST THERE. WE'RE...

...almost...

HAT THE DY HELL HAT?

GOOD GOD...

ALLAN, GET DOWN!

GET DOWN AND COVER YOUR EARS! HE'S GOING TO YELL...

hhhhhhhhh... hhrrRRRRRRR

...BASTA

CHRIST. HAS HE
FINISHED?

Um...

B-BREAD
AND TITS TO
YOU, FLASHING
MONSIGNOR.

BREAD AND
TITS TO YOU,
GILDED WASP
OF ELYSIUM.

LET THE
THRUP OF US
ENTENDER
WITHDOORS;
WHAT CHEER?

TH-THANK
YOU. THAT WOULD
BE LOVELY.

nng...

EM?

EM, ARE YOU HURT?

OH, BLOODY HELL. COME ON, LOVELY. YOU'RE ALL RIGHT, EH? YOU'RE ALL RIGHT...

buhh...

WHURR... WHWH HABBEN...?

THAT BLOODY COON'S DONE SOMETHING TO MY GOD-DAUGHTER.

LOOK AFTER HER. I'M GOING TO BOX HIS EARS.

BLOODY COON.

I WENCHED OUT ME BEAR-PIPE AND WHORLED HIM ALL 'ROUND...

...WITH A TRIPE OF MONSTABULARY KNACKED TO THE GROUND...

...THEN I SPANISHED TEN MERMALES UNTIL THEY'M WAS SORE...

I'M WILHELMINA MURRAY. I'VE SEEN OFF COUNT DRACULA, PROFESSOR JAMES MORIARTY AND THE MARTIAN INVASION OF 1898.

THIS IS MY COLLEAGUE, ALLAN QUATERMAIN.

QUATERMAIN.

GOD, IT *IS*, ISN'T IT? BUT *YOUNGER*. MY GOD...

THEY...THEY SAY YOU'RE BOTH TRAITORS, YOU KNOW.

WELL, THEY'D KNOW ABOUT TREACHERY, WOULDN'T THEY?

DID YOU KNOW IT WAS THE CURRENT "M" WHO HELPED ASSASSINATE BIG BROTHER?

N-NO. NO, I DIDN'T.

WELL, YOU DO NOW.

AND YOUR LITTLE LADYKILLER FRIEND JIMMY OUT THERE, HE'S BETRAYED THE WHOLE COUNTRY TO THE AMERICANS.

I'VE WORKED IT OUT.

THE AMERICANS WANTED JOHN NIGHT THE INDUSTRIALIST OUT OF THE WAY, BUT SO THEY COULDN'T BE HELD *RESPONSIBLE*.

JOHNNY *NIGHT?* WHAT ABOUT HIM?

DRUMMOND, COME *ON*. YOU'VE BEEN IN THIS GAME ALMOST AS LONG AS *WE* HAVE.

THE YANKS HAD ONE OF *OUR* AGENTS KILL NIGHT.

I.A.'S MR. *LEITER* EVEN ME HIM AN *ALIBI*.

AT THE TIME OF NIGHT'S DEATH, HE'D BE IN *JAMAICA*, FOILING AN ASIATIC *SCIENCE-VILLAIN*.

YOU KNOW, EVEN IN THE VILLAIN'S *CODENAME*, THE AMERICANS WERE LAUGHING AT US.

THERE WAS *NO DOCTOR*, MR. DRUMMOND.

ANYWAY, WE'RE LEAVING...

...GIVE OUR REGARDS TO THE DEPARTMENT, WON'T YOU?

Christ.

CHRIST, WHAT A FUCKIN' DUMP. AND WHAT'S THA' SMELL? IS THAT LINSEED OIL?

WHERE ARE THEY ALL, ANYWAY?

DID YOU GET THEM?

WH-WHAT THE FUCK WAS *THAT* FOR? I SWEAR I HAVEN'T *TOUCHED* HER...

GET UP.

WHAT...?

GET *UP*, YOU LITTLE *CUNT!*

I'M GOING TO MAKE YOU EAT YOUR OWN *SHIT* BEFORE I *FINISH* YOU!

NAAII...

YOU KILLED JOHNNY NIGHT FOR THE AMERICANS. FOR THE FUCKING *AMERICANS!*

HE WAS MY BEST MATE.

OH CHRIST. OH FUCKING HELL...

WHAT WAS IT, EH? SODIUM MORPHATE IN HIS FUCKING *PIE?*

YOU COWARDLY LITTLE BASTARD. IT'S ALWAYS *TRICKS* WITH YOU YOUNG FUCKERS, ISN'T IT?

AOHH...

TRICK *CARS,* TRICK *PENS,* TRICK *CIGARETTE LIGHTERS*...

WHY CAN'T YOU JUST *FIGHT?*

Ucch...

YOU ALL RIGHT?

UNNGH. HARDLY.

I'M GOING TO NEED STURDIER CLOTH- ING IF I STAY IN THIS BUSINESS.

WHERE IS EVERYBODY? WHERE'S UNCLE HUGO?

I'M...I'M SORRY.

THOSE COLD-BLOODED BASTARDS, THEY,...THEY KILLED HIM JUST BEFORE THEY ESCAPED.

THERE WAS NOTHING I COULD DO.

OH NO!

AN'T HAVE! UNCLE GO!

I--I HAVE TO SEE HIM...

NO, THAT'S NOT A GOOD IDEA.

LISTEN, HIS LAST THOUGHTS WERE OF YOU...

OH GOD.

OH, JIMMY...

SHH. IT'S ALL RIGHT.

IT'S ALL RIGHT.

I...I SUPPOSE IT'S WHAT HE'D HAVE WANTED, ISN'T IT?

TO GO OUT F-FIGHTING...

OF COURSE.

IN FACT, THOSE WERE HIS FINAL WORDS TO ME.

I WON'T RADIO THE 'COPTER FOR A WHILE.

WE CAN PROBABLY FIND AN INN NEARBY, WHERE YOU CAN RECOVER.

Th-THANK YOU.

THAT'S ALL RIGHT.

I SORT OF PROMISED YOUR UNCLE THAT I'D SEE TO YOU PROPERLY.

JIMMY, YOU'VE BEEN SO GOOD TO ME...

NOT AT ALL, M'LOVE.

NOT AT ALL.

Mmm. THIS IS SUPER, ISN'T IT?

WELL, IT'S BETTER THAN THAT BLOODY ROCKET.

ANY IDEA HOW LONG BEFORE WE GET THERE, YOUR MAJESTY?

HO HO! FAIR JOCKO TO YE, MASTER Q! YE'VE KEPT IN YER MUZZ HOW I BE KING O' PANKY-WANK!

WE'LL HANG HOMELIGHTS AFARE LONG.

GOOD. IT'S BEEN SO LONG SINCE I'VE SEEN THE BLAZING WORLD THAT I'VE ALMOST FORGOTTEN WHAT IT LOOKS LIKE.

AN ORLA WILL THER

HEER ORLANDO IS MOMENTEEL EEN DAME.

WHAT DID SHE SAY? AND IS THAT PEG OR SARAH JANE?

THAT'S PEG. PEG'S TALLER...

...AND I THINK SHE SAID THAT ORLANDO'S CURRENTLY FEMALE.

THAT WOULD BE NICE, WOULDN'T IT?

I'LL SAY.

THESE DOLLS ARE MARVELLOUS, AREN'T THEY?

AYE. THE AND THEY THRUP O SASTERS

THEY'M KEPT ME OX-BOLT LARDY SINC FORST I BECEIVED 'EM.

WAS THAT WHEN YOU ARRIVED HERE?

FORST HITHERED FRO ME DARKLY-SUBSTANCED HOME-WHIRL LUNDERED I IN TOY-LEND.

Ah, SO QUEEN OLYMPIA PRESENTED YOU WITH THE DOLLS?

WIJ HEBBEN ONS VRIJWILLIG AANGEBODEN. ZIJN GESLACHT IS KOLOSSAAL.

WHAT DID SHE SAY?

SHE, UM, SHE SAYS THEY VOLUNTEERED BECAUSE OF HIS PERSONALITY.

SO, ABOUT THIS VESSEL...

I MEAN, ARE THESE THINGS COMMON IN YOUR BLACK-MATERIAL COSMOS?

THESE CRAFTS THAT SAIL BETWEEN DIMENSIONS?

CUMMUN? WHY, BLISS YER SLAP, NO.

TED "THE ROSE O' WHERE" ALL ON ME JINGLE, DID I.

THER GALLEY-WAGS D AS IT'D NAILWISE BE DUNNED.

WHAT SQUINT, SAREY JANE?

IK DENK DAT DIE GROTE WOLK DAAR DE WEG NAAR HUIS IS.

IS THAT VERRIBLE?

WELL, IN THAT STAMP I'D BEST PAW OUT THE QUIZGOGS.

WHAT DID SHE SAY? ARE WE NEARLY THERE?

AYE—SO, THROUGH THE BIG CLODDER AHEAVE O' WE.

THUNCE WE SHALL REQUEER OUR BLINK-WEAR...

SE. MY, THAT IS A BIG CLOUD. AND VERY TWINKLY, TOO.

DO YOU NEED ANY HELP WITH THOSE, DARLING?

O. I'M NE.

THERE. WHAT ABOUT THE DOLLS? WILL THEY BE ABLE TO SEE?

OH, DON'T YOU'M FRIZZLE ABOUT THEY. THEY'M MOCKINICAL.

YOU'M JUST PEER OFFLY...

THARBLO.

HUFF YER OVVER IN ALL YOU'M TICK SENNED SUCH A PLUMIOUS SPARKTACLE?

OH, JUST ABOUT EVERYBODY... ALTHOUGH THE CAPTAIN'S TIED UP OVERHAULING *THE NAUTILUS* AND SAID YOU'D BEST VISIT THE SUB-MARINE PENS FOR AN AUDIENCE.

FAIR ENOUGH, I SUPPOSE. TELL NEMO THAT WE'LL BE DOWN LATER.

Y'KNOW, THIS PLACE LOOKS *DIFFERENT* TO HOW I REMEMBER IT, ALTHOUGH IN A TIMELESS WAY, IT'S EXACTLY THE *SAME*.

WELL, WHAT ABOUT THESE *PORTALS?* I'M SURE *THEY'RE* NEW.

OH, HAVEN'T YOU SEEN THOSE? THEY'RE RATHER GOOD. THEY'RE APERTURES INTO ALL THE OVERLAPPING DIMENSIONS THAT THE BLAZING WORLD *CONNECTS* TO.

I THINK *THESE* LEAD SIMULTANEOUSLY TO THE SWINE-THINGS' *BORDERLAND* AND THE VARIOUS REALMS OF THAT PECULIAR TREE IN BUCKINGHAMSHIRE.

APPARENTLY, THE TRICK IS TO CLOSE ONE EYE THEN THE OTHER, SO THAT YOU CAN SEE THE COEXISTENT ZONES *SEPARATELY.*

THAT'S JOLLY CLEVER. YOU KNOW, I'VE LOVED THE BLAZING WORLD EVER SINCE WE FIRST CAME HERE IN... 1907, WAS IT?

WELL, WE *SAW* IT THEN, WE DIDN'T ACTUA COME ASHORE U SOME YEARS LATER.

I AGREE, THOUGH. IT'S MARVELOUS *HID AWAY* FOR US, YOU GET TO ME AN ALTOGETHE BETTER SORT O PERSON.

FOR TRULY IS OUR CAVALCADE NOW DONE, OUR BEAD-GAME WON, OUR RADIANT SYNTHESIS COMPLETE, ITS FIGURES AND ITS ARABESQUES RESOLVED BELOW THIS ROARING FIRMAMENT.

THIS SHINING SOIL BEYOND LIFE'S MUMMIED GRIP, FAR PAST THE MAUL OF FACT, WHERE THOUGHTS PARADE.

OUR DIREST YEARNINGS AND OUR FONDEST FEARS AT SPORT, MADE SAFE FROM TIME'S INIQUITY.

WE ARE THE TALES THAT SOOTHED YOUR INFANT BROW, THE ROLES YOU WORE FOR CHILDHOOD'S ALLEY-PLAY.

DID NOT YOUR YOUTH, WHEN LUST EACH NOTION SEIZED, SEE PAPER PARAMOUR TOOK OFT TO BED?

WHEN GROWN TO GREY RESPONSIBILITY, ITS DISENCHANTMENTS AND DIURNAL TOILS, COME EACH DAY'S DISAPPOINTED END WERE WE NOT ALL THY CONSOLATION, THY ESCAPE?

AND MORE, THE VERY PERSONALITY THAT SCRYS THIS EPILOGUE WAS ONCE UNFORMED, ASSEMBLED HASTILY FROM BORROWED SCRAPS, FROM TRAITS ADMIRED IN OTHERS, FROM IDEALS.

DID FICTIONAL EXAMPLES NOT PREVAIL? HOLMES' INTELLECT? THE MIGHT OF HERCULES? OUR VIRTUES, OUR INTOXICATING VICE: WHILE FASHIONING THYSELF, WERE THESE NOT CLAY?

IF WE MERE INSUBSTANTIAL FANCIES BE, HOW MORE SO THEE, WHO FROM US SUBSTANCE STOLE?

INTANGIBLE, WE ARE LIFE'S SECRET SOUL. ITS GUIDING LANTERN PRINCIPLE, ITS BEST. UNTARNISHED BY ALL SUBTERFUGE OR SPIES, UNSHACKLED FROM MUNDANE AUTHORITIES.

LIFE'S CERTAINTIES ERODE, YET WE ENDURE. WHILST TYRANTS TOPPLE, YET QUIXOTE RIDES WITH THE COMPANIONS OF THY CRADLE NIGHTS IN GLORIOUS PASTURE COLERIDGE NEVER GLIMPSED.

NOT THOU ALONE, BUT ALL HUMANITY [B]OTH IN ITS PROGRESS [A]BLE EMULATE. WHENCE [C]AME THY ROCKET-SHIPS [A]ND SUBMARINES IF NOT [F]ROM NAUTILUS, FROM CAVORITE?

YOUR TRUSTIEST COMPANIONS SINCE THE CAVE, WE APPARITIONS GUIDED MANKIND'S TREAD, OUR PLANET, UNSEEN COUNTERPART TO THINE, AS PERMANENT, AS VEN'RABLE, AS TRUE.

ON DREAM'S [FO]UNDATION MATTER'S [SH]IPYARDS REST. TWO [TOU]CHING HANDS, EACH [THE] OTHER DRAWS: [THE F]ANTASIES THOU'VE [FA]SHIONED FASHION THEE.

REJOICE! IMAGINATION'S QUENCHLESS PYRE BURNS ON, A BEACON TO ETERNITY, ITS TRIUMPHS CULTURE'S PROUDEST PINNACLES WHEN GREAT WARS ARE INGLORIOUSLY FORGOT.

HERE IS OUR NARRATIVE MADE PARADISE, BRIEF TALES MADE GLORIOUS CONTINUITY. HERE CHAMPIONS AND LOVERS ARE MADE SAFE FROM BOWDLERIZER'S QUILL, OR FAD, OR FACT.

HERE ARE BRAVE BANNERS OF *ROMANCE* UNFURLED...